Flavors from the Garden

Heirloom Vegetable Recipes from Roughwood

Flavors from the Garden

Heirloom Vegetable Recipes from Roughwood

William Woys Weaver

Photographs by Noah Fecks

RIZZOLI
NEW YORK

New York · Paris · London · Milan

For Valerie

Flavors from the Garden

Heirloom Vegetable Recipes from Roughwood

First published in the United States of America in 2021 by
Rizzoli International Publications, Inc.
300 Park Avenue South
New York, NY 10010
rizzoliusa.com

Photography by Noah Fecks
noahfecks.com

Design: Jennifer S. Muller
jennifermullerdesign.com

Publisher: Charles Miers
Editor: Jono Jarrett
Production Manager: Kaija Markoe
Managing Editor: Lynn Scrabis

Printed in China
2021 2022 2023 2024 / 10 9 8 7 6 5 4 3 2 1

ISBN: 978-0-8478-7079-0
Library of Congress Control Number: 2021934013

Visit us online:
Facebook.com/RizzoliNewYork
Twitter: @Rizzoli_Books
Instagram.com/RizzoliBooks
Pinterest.com/RizzoliBooks
Youtube.com/user/RizzoliNY
Issuu.com/Rizzoli

Contents

Introduction

The Roughwood Table

Many years ago, while still a teenager, I experienced a profound culinary epiphany after reading Esther Aresty's, *The Delectable Past*. An insatiable collector of old cookbooks, she celebrated those forgotten worlds captured between the covers, culling recipes from her favorites to prove her journey of discovery was both philosophical and practical. From the wise advice of Carême, who created the architecture of food as performance, to the obsessive New England orderliness of Mrs. Lincoln's *Boston Cook Book*, many relevant and applicable lessons are still to be found here, as I have learned myself from a lifetime of collecting. Just as the calligrapher transforms ink into art, so too the gardener and then the cook gather, prepare, and utilize basic ingredients that will determine the dynamics of any recipe. Classic cookery—great cookery—is not born out of novelty but from a special communication with ingredients. That basic truism defines this book (and to be honest all my books), since these pages represent a culinary journey through the kitchen garden at Roughwood, first laid out in 1805 when the property began operation as The Lamb Tavern. Safe to say, that venerable garden with all its inherited culinary spirits has assumed a life of its own.

Perhaps it is not purely by accident that this book begins and ends with two rustic bean soups: On one hand, early spring finds the Coco de Paimpol (a white soup bean) and the *Petit Carré de Caen* (a white cut-short bean) starting off our recipe journey by way of a delightful Breton-style *cotriade*, but one without fish. In the last chapter, the *haricot Tarbais* lima bean provides us with another meaning of cassoulet as only regional French cooking can express it in all its well-deserved cultural diversity. Garden vegetables and mushrooms take the place of fish or meat in both dishes, although both dishes share the same French cultural penchant for unique, flavorful white beans.

Part of my culinary mantra is that fresh ingredients, which define what we are as humans, also define our food. We are sometimes intentionally ambiguous about the fact that our personal foodways may ultimately define our life's outcome because it does not match expectations, but tough love to say, they do. So, this book is not about how to live a long life on hopeful expectations, but simply how

to take life day to day and to appreciate it in all its fleeting richness. Each recipe is designed to help you find that happy place; some require work, but so do relationships, so cookery reflects real life, and I will never dismiss the idea that one is good training for the other.

Many of the recipes included in this book feature some of that creative adaptation from archaic to modern without losing respect for the past. Our seed collection has been called "the Walden Pond of heirloom seeds" because Roughwood is both a philosophy and an undertaking with a practical objective. That is why the gardener in me has always been drawn to cookery books that go beyond the recipe. One of my perennial favorites is John Evelyn's 1699 *Acetaria. A Discourse of Sallets*, possibly the first book of its kind devoted entirely to salads. His recipes always startle and challenge, until you make them and discover what a genius he was when it came to flavor and the unique spirituality that comes from understanding plants because you have grown them. Evelyn was wealthy enough to explore esoteric greens with all the passion of a perfectionist. He found usefulness in seemingly worthless plants and despised waste; we are soul brothers on that point.

Not to be outdone by modern statisticians, he even published a chart listing all the popular salad greens of his day, how to cultivate them, and when to harvest, and what parts of the plants are most useful in the kitchen. There is nothing stale about his advice and his recipe for pickling purslane would be as trendy today as when he first wrote it. Like Evelyn's treatise, *Flavors from the Garden* is also vegetable-centric and tries to give plants their just dues, and while not vegan or even strictly vegetarian in every dish, the underlying idea is to give rare—beautiful, delicious, and wholesome—heirloom vegetables their rightful place. I take inspiration from the enterprising work of past generations for whom thoughtfully plotted kitchen gardens and seasonal eating were everyday facts of life. In some ways, my book echoes William Salmon's 1710 *Family Dictionary*, the go-to cookbook for Philadelphia's old Quaker elites, and *Adam's Luxury, and Eve's Cookery*, published in 1744. Both books were written by part-time gardeners but intended for the full-time kitchen—not too different in their purpose than the book you are now reading. While the latter title may evoke Eden and the idea that a plant-based diet is indeed the healthiest, it is not vegetarian, although animal products play a secondary role. This is close to what many recommend today, and while eighteenth-century recipes are often heavy on salted butter and spices, it is possible to adapt many of *Eve*'s dishes while relishing their surprisingly up-to-date spirit.

Another and far more contemporary formative inspiration for this book was the late British food writer, Jane Grigson, whose 1978 *Jane Grigson's Vegetable Book* and many subsequent transatlantic conversations helped me redefine the gardens at Roughwood. She gave me hope when I thought the weeds were winning. "Cook them," advised she, "they're good for you." She was right. Eating the weeds is a first rule of maintaining a kitchen garden—dandelions, purslane, and even lowly sow's thistle are free as well as nutrient rich. In an ideal world there are no weeds, just things we eat. In Jane Grigson's world, good deeds, philosophy, and food blended into one important message. We both loved Evelyn's *Acetaria* but also had something else in common: a birthday, March 13. That connection, or Pisces karma, forged a special bond. When she passed on March 12, 1990, one day before our shared birthday, the garden world lost a kindred spirit. Happily, her daughter Sophie Grigson is now carrying the torch as a food writer.

I am sure Jane would be excited by this book's devotion to the vegetable-centric themes of Evelyn and *Adam's Luxury*, not to mention reviving the tradition of the soup bunch, an ingenious component of early American cookery. "Soup bunch" is now a very old-fashioned term for a bundle of vegetables and herbs poached in water to create stock or added to a stock to impart richer flavor. Where a bouquet garni traditionally includes sprigs of parsley, thyme, and bay leaf, the soup bunch is more substantial and larger in size, most often including aromatics such as onions, carrots, and celery, but also turnip or rutabaga, cabbage, tomatoes, or greens. It was often tailored to regions, seasons, or preference. A classic of the genre, the Charleston Soup Bunch traditionally comprises sliced squash, green onions, parsley, a carrot, baby parsnips, thyme, dill, and celery stalks. Several classic examples of a Philadelphia soup bunch feature in the still life paintings of early-1800s Raphaelle Peale. Industrialized agriculture and an overall decline in kitchen gardens have largely reduced soup bunches to quaint references, but perhaps surprisingly, you can still find packaged combinations in supermarkets or even from grocery delivery services. In this book, I employ soup bunches in some recipes where vegetable stock is called for but also where I have intentionally eliminated meat or fish stock. The soup bunch is perhaps most effective when added to unsalted broth left over from poaching

vegetables, greatly amplifying the flavor of the stock. Soup bunches can be employed to create specific flavor profiles, such as where salsify stands in for oyster broth in a vegetarian Breton bean soup (page 14). The soup bunch needs rediscovery because it reminds us of how much we can make from very little. Beyond soup bunches and philosophical conundrums, this book is divided into four chapters, so that each is devoted to one season and what the culinary biodiversity of a well-plotted kitchen garden produces. Each recipe represents a journey through time and the passage of the sun as well as a journey through flavors new or rediscovered. Recipes feature interesting heirlooms such as Chrysanthemum Melons, *coztomatls*, New Guinea Basil, Almagro Eggplants, Spaghetti Peppers, and Wild Muskmelons. From Roughwood itself, Seed Collection Manager Stephen Smith and I hope a few new varieties created here will find a home in your community garden or backyard plot, such as Wandering Spirits Corn, Ginger Crunch Dahlia, and Roughwood Green Glaze Collards. We are proud to maintain the largest collection of Native American corn, squash, and beans in this country, to secure these seeds for posterity outside of politics and for Native American populations in particular. For this reason, I am partial to the rare Gaspé Flint Corn (see page 159), a miniature heirloom variety that can be grown in a flowerpot.

We have fairies at Roughwood; even the nonbelievers have seen and heard them. When the Green Corn Moon illuminates the garden with its brilliant August light, and the Gaspé corn is in full tassel, we experience the joyous rhythms of Mother Nature as the wee folk dance in their circles. Our social mandate is to help you feed your families. Beyond that, for your own culinary growth and in order to take control of what you eat and who determines it, experimenting with heirloom seeds can open your eyes to foods you never knew existed. We hope that these cultural treasures can become tools for you to stay healthy and centered on your family and its well-being.

Garden epiphanies defined the spirit of my book, *Heirloom Vegetable Gardening*, which in turn proved a remarkable inspiration for many people who have decided to grow their own food. I receive that feedback all the time. This book takes those ideas that one step farther, because the joy of gardening does not end with a wheelbarrow full of produce. It's what comes next, magical transformations in the kitchen and larder, and how they bring the cycle of life to the table.

William Woys Weaver,
Epicure with Hoe
Roughwood

Spring

An Ode to Rhubarb

On those magical but rare occasions in Pennsylvania Dutch country when the February full moon appears on Stag Monday (which is the Monday before Shrove Tuesday), the *Buschmops* takes flight in the sky in the form of a white stag with antlers of gold. The *Buschmops* is the name of the woodland fairy, according to Pennsylvania Dutch tradition, who is lord of the forests and all wild beasts. When he transforms himself into a white stag, flecks of gold rain down from his antlers; where this enchanted dust strikes the earth, snowdrops appear in full bloom.

The *Buschmops* often leaves a massive trail of snowdrops in the gardens at Roughwood, although spring on our part of Devon Hill arrives in distinct stages. It begins in the walled garden once dominated by an ancient white oak; the Cornelian cherries then burst forth in frilly yellow, followed westward by other spring flowers. As wild honeybees work the snowdrops, doubtless hungry from their long winter hibernation, other slumbering plants come alive—first Shepherd's Purse, then Upland Cress, followed by Catawissa Onions, Spinach Leaf Beets, hardy lettuces, nettles, and the tentative unfolding leaves of Early Champagne Rhubarb. It is always the first rhubarb to appear, apple green and about as close to gooseberries in flavor as can be. Next comes Victoria, the classic thick-stemmed red rhubarb created in 1837 (and perhaps the genetic mother or grandmother of most of the commercial rhubarbs grown today). The rarest one arrives last: my grandfather's Strawberry Rhubarb,

which never runs to seed and produces strawberry-red stems all summer long. One variety I miss is Pineapple Rhubarb, which my grandfather obtained during the 1920s from Henry Buckwalter Weaver, a distant cousin in Lancaster County, who operated greenhouses in East Lampeter with his brother, B. Ellis Weaver. Its brilliant yellow stems were slightly sweet, with a hint of tropical fruit flavor, hence the name. We lost it during a drought and have never been able to locate replacements.

Most of our rhubarbs show signs of life by Saint Gertrude's Day, March 17, which for the Pennsylvania Dutch is the traditional beginning of spring, Saint Gertrude being the patron saint of kitchen gardens. She is also the guardian of the *Eckleit*, the fairies who live in the corners of gardens and the reason many Dutch still plant flowers there, to insure a happy harvest. We used to plant sweet violets (*Viola odorata*) in several of the corners because by Easter they filled the air with their distinctive perfume and then bloomed again in November. While the deer enjoyed the violets, the *Eckleit* prefer bee plants, so there is now no shortage of zinnias, dahlias, cleomes, and four-o-clocks all summer long to keep the fairies happy.

Piles of rhubarb soon invade the kitchen, signaling it is time to embark on a flurry of conserves, marmalades, relishes, and my favorite spring treat, Parsnip-Rhubarb Soup (page 36). My great-grandmother used to make it every spring and probably came across the novel flavor combination while enrolled in Mrs. Rorer's Philadelphia Cooking School in the late 1880s. Whatever the case, rhubarb-parsnip soup so outshines vichyssoise I am led to wonder why this uniquely flavored delicacy is not more popular—I suspect the issue starts with parsnips, which are sadly underutilized and yet bless the kitchen garden with spring abundance, if only you manage to dig them before they start to bolt. Bolting means the parsnips have begun to grow again and thus send up a central shoot. This causes the roots to turn woody and worthless, unless you want to use them in a soup bunch. Winter freezing does not harm parsnips, and there are many gardeners like me who firmly believe that a good frost improves their flavor. You can tell they are good by the way they smell when you lift them: sweet and aromatic. I always associate digging parsnips with snipping spring chives, as the two flavors seem married to one another, which is why chives will always enhance the flavor of parsnips, no matter how long you cook them.

The other recipes in this section of the book may spark your creativity with an array of edible plants generally overlooked during spring garden cleanup. Nettles are not invasive (they are related to mint) when viewed as ingredients for pies, herbal teas, or even soup. And while the window for wild-harvesting ramps may be short, for us in Pennsylvania they are a late April celebration that can be captured in pesto and then frozen for year-round enjoyment. And don't sleep on Upland Cress. It is easy to grow, reseeds itself readily, and will supply all the same culinary and health benefits as watercress. Its high vitamin C content inspired the nickname "scurvy grass." With fresh food now available every hour of the day, one might easily forget the destitution people once suffered for lack of healthy food during early spring, before the summer garden was planted. A kitchen garden wisely managed can supply the table with a surprising array of choices even in lean months, as I hope these recipes demonstrate.

Bean Soup with Salsify and Oyster Mushrooms

This hearty two-bean soup celebrates salsify and spring leeks, as well as two heirloom beans: *Haricot Paimpolais de Guyader* from Paimpol and the Haricot Petit Carré de Caen—called carré because it is a cut-short bean with square corners due to crowding in the pods. Both are white; the Paimpol bush bean is large and meaty, while the Caen pole bean is small and delicate.

For salsify, I prefer the variety called *Lüthi*, taking its name from the Swiss farmer who preserved it for posterity. Once cleaned of dirt, salsify resembles a thin, pearly-white parsnip; its flavor is sometimes likened to oysters but also resembles artichokes and celeriac. If you are growing your own leeks, then you will want good overwintering varieties for early spring harvest. I recommend the hardy Giant Musselburgh, *Bleu de Solaise*, or the *Long de Mézières* winter leek. And do not skimp on the chervil: its unique flavor gives this soup a classic touch.

Serves 6 to 8

1½ cups dried Coco de Paimpol or large white cannellini bean

1 cup dried *Haricot Petit Carré de Caen* or small white bean

Sea salt

1 lemon

1 pound fresh salsify roots, trimmed and washed

2 tablespoons all-purpose flour

4 tablespoons unsalted butter

1 large leek, washed, trimmed, and chopped (white parts only)

2 quarts vegetable stock enhanced with a soup bunch (see page 193)

4 large fresh bay leaves, gently bruised to release flavor

2 large garlic cloves, finely minced or passed through a garlic press

2 teaspoons fresh thyme leaves, or to taste

4 ounces oyster mushrooms, stemmed and chopped

2 tablespoons minced chervil, or to taste

2 tablespoons minced parsley, or to taste

Freshly ground white pepper

Chopped chives, for garnish

In a deep bowl, cover the dried beans with boiling water by at least 1 inch. Cover and let soak at least 3 to 4 hours or overnight, until they double in size. Drain off any remaining liquid, rinse the beans, and transfer to a deep stewing pan. Cover with 3 quarts fresh water and season lightly with salt. Bring to a rolling boil over medium-high heat, then reduce heat and simmer until the beans are tender, about 30 minutes. Drain and set aside in a clean stewing pan.

Halve the lemon, juice into a large bowl of cool water, and add the squeezed halves. Peel the skin from the salsify and immediately plunge into the lemon water (otherwise the roots will turn an unsightly brown). While paring the salsify, heat 1 quart of water in a deep stewing pan over medium heat and whisk in the flour. Bring to a slow boil and cook 2 minutes, then add the salsify and poach until tender—this classic white poaching stock is my preferred way to tenderize the salsify. Drain, rinse quickly in cold water, pat dry with paper towels, then slice the roots thinly on the bias and set aside.

In a broad saucepan, melt the butter over medium heat and add the leeks. Cover and sweat over a medium heat until the leeks are soft (about 6 minutes). Remove from the heat and puree in a food processor or blender with 1 quart stock until smooth. Pour the leek mixture over the beans and add the remaining 1 quart stock, bay leaves, garlic, and thyme. Bring this to a gentle boil over a medium heat. Once the soup is steaming hot, add the sliced salsify and mushrooms. Cook 5 minutes until heated through, then add the chervil and parsley, and season with salt and white pepper. Serve immediately garnished liberally with chopped chives.

Haricot Petit Carré

It is worth mentioning that Slow Food France has taken special interest in the *Haricot Petit Carré*. We have been growing this rare heirloom bean for many years without realizing its historical importance. The bean was first noticed by horticulturalists at Château de Fontaine-Henry near Bayeux in 1844, but the owner of the property said at the time that the bean originated at the old Prémontré Abbey of Ardenne. Its history traces at least to the eighteenth century, since the abbey was disbanded and sold in 1791. This unique bean began to disappear from commerce in the 1960s, falling victim during the shift to hybrids, but it is now undergoing a revival as an artisanal cultivar. The Bretons cook it while still green in the pod as a shelling bean as well as a dry bean. It is a classic in soup.

Chickweed Pie

Chickweed (*Stellaria media*) is often considered the bane of spring gardens, yet it is also an old-time medical plant very high in nutritional value. To me, old-fashioned Pennsylvania Dutch chickweed pie is one of the rites of passage of spring. Of course, it goes well with wine, a little Prosecco for the stomach's sake, so why not enjoy Nature's gift even if the rest of the world considers it a weed? As a substitute for chickweed, use 4 cups of finely chopped spinach or a combination of spinach and chard. You can also make this with nettles (see Note, page 30) or other wild greens.

A few words about harvesting chickweed: since the plant grows flat against the ground, you must pick through it for twigs and leaves. Trim off the root ends of the stems, reserving only the greenest and leafiest parts of the plant. Rinse thoroughly in a colander, then pat dry with paper towels. Gather into a ball and then chop it with a sharp knife much as you would mince an onion. Or process in a food processor until reduced to confetti texture. Measure out 3 cups and proceed with the recipe. I take a shortcut and use a purchased piecrust, but use your favorite pastry.

Serves 6 to 8

3 cups finely chopped chickweed or spinach (see Note)

1 prepared piecrust, rolled out to a 14-inch round

1 cup diced slab bacon

½ cup finely chopped onion

3 large eggs (duck eggs, if you can get them)

1½ cups sour cream

1 tablespoon all-purpose flour

½ teaspoon freshly grated nutmeg

Sea salt and freshly ground black pepper

Once cleaned and chopped, set the chickweed aside in a large bowl. Preheat the oven to 325°F. Line a 10-inch pie plate with the piecrust. Fold over and crimp along the edge to keep the filling from running over, and set aside. Fry the diced bacon in a skillet over medium heat until it begins to brown, then add the onion. Cover and sweat until the onion is soft, about 3 minutes. Using a slotted spoon, add the onion and bacon mixture to the chickweed. Reserve the drippings for another use, if desired (see page 162).

In a separate bowl, beat the eggs until a lemon color then add the sour cream, flour, and nutmeg. Add the mixture to the chickweed, incorporate well, and season with salt and pepper. Spread the mixture evenly in the prepared pie shell and pat down firmly with the back of a spoon. Bake until the pie is cooked in the center and has developed a golden tinge across the top, about 1 hour. Serve hot or at room temperature.

Saint Gertrude's Day Salad with Rhubarb Dressing

While the rest of the country goes green for Saint Patrick on March 17, we in the Pennsylvania Dutch country prefer to commemorate Saint Gertrude. As a Celtic fertility goddess transformed into an early Catholic saint, she is older and much more formidable, and as the maternal patron of kitchen gardens and cats, she is also far more effective in the early spring garden. I've found this crisp salad is excellent served with chilled rosé or Champagne.

Saint Gertrude's day is also the date when we turn over the soil, bring in fresh compost or manure, and begin the process of planting potatoes, onions, and spring greens. In a season when many gardens appear barren, closer inspection reveals gleanings aplenty. Dandelions, corn salad, garden cress, shepherd's purse, miniature radicchios (including my favorites, *Grumolo verde* and *Grumolo rossa*), mustard greens, frilly Katie's Mustard Lettuce, variegated winter cress, robust cold-hardy lettuces like speckled *Salade de Russie*, even delicate *Viola labradorica* with its edible purple-tinged leaves—all vie for a place on the early spring menu.

Serves 6 to 8

8 ounces mixed early spring greens of your choice (see Note)

½ cup chopped walnuts or hickory nuts, toasted

½ cup dried strawberries or raspberries

Rhubarb Dressing (recipe follows)

Gently wash the greens and dry in a salad spinner. Arrange the greens in a large bowl or platter.

Scatter the chopped nuts and dried berries over the top and mix. Serve, passing the dressing separately so guests may add to taste.

RHUBARB DRESSING

This pale pink dressing complements not only spring greens, but also crudités, steamed broccoli, boiled potatoes, and even fresh strawberries.

Makes 3 cups

12 ounces fresh rhubarb (3 large stems)

4 ounces red onion (about ½ medium) cut in half lengthwise, then sliced paper-thin

¾ cup tarragon vinegar or champagne vinegar

½ cup extra-virgin olive oil or shallot-flavored oil (see Confit recipe, following page)

4 ounces shallots or St. John's shallots, coarsely chopped

8 ounces silken tofu

2 tablespoons poppy seeds

2 tablespoons dried mint, crumbled

1 tablespoon sugar

2 teaspoons sea salt

Grated zest of half a lemon, or to taste

Peel the red skin from each rhubarb stem and transfer the peels to a sterilized jar, reserving and refrigerating the peeled stems. Add the sliced onion to the rhubarb skins and cover with the vinegar. Transfer to the refrigerator and infuse for at least 24 hours, or until the vinegar is tinted bright red. Strain the vinegar into a bowl and set aside, discarding the skins and onion.

In a small sauté pan, heat the oil over medium until just shimmering and add the shallots. Cover and sweat over medium heat until softened, about 4 minutes. While the shallots are cooking, chop the peeled reserved rhubarb stems. Once the shallots are soft, add the sliced rhubarb, cover, and cook until the rhubarb is soft, about 6 minutes. Remove from the heat and cool to room temperature.

Once cool, transfer the shallot-rhubarb mixture and cooking oil to a food processor or blender and puree until smooth. Add the infused vinegar and the tofu. Puree until the dressing is smooth and creamy, then transfer to a clean bowl.

Stir in the poppy seeds, mint, sugar, and salt, and taste to adjust seasoning. Add the lemon zest, a little at a time according to taste. Let the dressing mature for an hour or two before serving. Dressing will keep in the refrigerator for up to 1 week but is best on the day it's made.

Confit of St. John's Shallots

Saint John's shallots are not true shallots, rather something unique halfway between onions and garlic. They resemble large red shallots but, unlike shallots and onions, which are planted in the spring, they must be planted in the late summer or early fall for harvest the following year. This "vernalizing" process (undergoing the cold of winter) is what separates them from the onion tribe and provides them with a kinship to garlic, which also must be vernalized. This weird situation is the result of unique genetics: the Saint John's shallot is triploid, which means it evolved from three parents instead of two. This remarkable birth took place in the Himalayas and has always been imbued with a special curative reputation. In fact, this recipe was originally administered to invalids and the sick.

Perceived medical properties aside, Saint John's shallot is also better than true shallots in cookery, due to its uniquely intense flavor. Confit is one of the easiest and most versatile ways to keep them on hand as a condiment.

Makes 6 cups

2 pounds St. John's shallots or large red shallots, trimmed and peeled

20 fresh bay leaves

6 sprigs thyme, preferably spiked thyme (*Thymbra spicata*)

2½ to 3 cups extra-virgin olive oil

Preheat the oven to 325°F. Pack the shallots in one layer in a shallow baking pan or casserole, preferably with a lid. Tuck the bay leaves evenly among the shallots and scatter the thyme evenly on top. Cover with enough oil to submerge the shallots, then cover with the lid or cover tightly with foil. Bake until the shallots are very soft and golden-red, 1½ to 2 hours. Serve hot or at room temperature.

Confit will keep in an airtight container in the refrigerator for up to 3 weeks. Once the shallots have been eaten, the flavorful oil also makes an excellent base for cooking or salad dressing.

Grass Pea Omelet

The Cyprus Grass Pea—also called Cyprus Vetch—has been misidentified by many horticulturalists as a chickling vetch (*Lathyrus sativus*), and even several trusted books on Mediterranean flora list it as such. In fact, the varietal locally called louvana is a different species altogether (*Lathyrus orchus*). Cypriot cuisine makes broad use of their grass pea and there are many landraces: a brown-eyed variety from Arminou (*louvana mavromati*), a gray-seeded variety, and even a black one. We have been growing all of these at Roughwood because the plants are easy to cultivate and are notably prolific, both in terms of pea yields and in the amount of delicate young greens suitable for spring omelets. Even its flowers are edible.

Louvana can be planted early like true garden peas and it will reseed for a fall harvest. In some parts of Cyprus where there is no real frost during the winter, this pea supplies garden greens from October through April. The dry seeds resemble yellow split peas and can be used in recipes like any typical culinary split pea. For omelets, choose only the youngest sprouts with tender leaves. Stems may be tough and stringy, and are best discarded.

Serves 2 to 4

3 tablespoons extra-virgin olive oil or sesame oil

1 small onion, cut in half lengthwise, then sliced paper-thin

2 garlic cloves, minced

1 bunch fresh louvana, coarsely chopped

3 large eggs

Sea salt and freshly ground black pepper

Lightly crushed cumin and coriander seeds, to taste

In a broad, shallow pan, heat the oil over medium just until starting to smoke. Add the onion and garlic, stir to coat, and cover. Sweat the onions until soft, for about 4 minutes then add the louvana. Cover and cook until bright green, another 4 minutes.

Beat the eggs until light and frothy. Once the greens are cooked, remove the lid and drizzle the eggs over the vegetables. Cook until lightly browned on the bottom, 3 to 4 minutes. Carefully flip the omelet and brown the other side, about another 3 minutes. Sprinkle with salt, pepper, cumin, and coriander to taste and serve immediately.

Parsnip Curd

Fresh homemade fruit or vegetable curd is one of those classic Quaker foods that my grandmother grew up making for picnics and special occasions, one that now seems to have faded from the scene. When I discovered I could make it with parsnips (and lower the cholesterol by cutting down on eggs), it became a natural use for my spring surplus. This is a perfect spread for sliced pound cake or used as a filling in small tarts. It can also be served with almond cookies or parsnip biscuits (recipe opposite). No one will ever guess it's made from parsnips! Let the curd sit for 1 day before serving for best flavor.

Makes 2 cups

1 pound parsnips (about 4 medium), peeled and sliced into 2-inch pieces

1⅔ cups sugar

5 tablespoons fresh lemon juice

1½ tablespoons freshly grated lemon zest

2 tablespoons unsalted butter

In a small saucepan, cover the parsnips with water and bring to a boil over medium-high heat. Cook until tender, 20 to 25 minutes. Drain and let cool. Transfer the cooked parsnips to a food processor and puree until smooth and creamy, about 1½ minutes.

Transfer to a broad, shallow saucepan and add the sugar, lemon juice, lemon zest, and butter. Cook over a medium-low heat, stirring constantly until the mixture attains the consistency of applesauce, about 15 to 20 minutes. Transfer to glass jars, cover with a lid, and let cool. Curd will keep in the refrigerator up to 7 days.

Parsnip Biscuits

It was a cold, rainy day in March when I first stumbled on this recipe. I had just come in from the garden muddy, blue at the fingertips but well supplied with a basket of freshly dug parsnips when a package of rare old cookbooks arrived. Among them was Hannah Bouvier Peterson's *National Cook Book* from 1850, a trove of old Philadelphia Quaker recipes. Peterson, an astronomer at heart, was related to the famous confectioner Elizabeth Goodfellow (through one of Elizabeth's several husbands) as well as to cook and confectioner Hannah Widdifield, adding yet another complex genealogical dimension to Philadelphia's remarkable culinary portrait.

Using parsnips instead of potatoes to set a sponge is an altogether clever baking concept, especially since the heavy clay soils where I live encourage parsnips to perfection. In fact, old time farmers planted parsnips to "break up" the fields in preparation for more profitable crops. With a fresh pot of tea, these biscuits are a spiritual cure for any cold, stormy spring day. Serve them hot directly from the oven with Parsnip Curd (recipe opposite).

Makes about 32 biscuits

1 medium parsnip (about 4 ounces), peeled and cut into 1-inch pieces

1¼-ounce package dry yeast

1⅓ cups milk, heated to 105°F

4¼ cups bread flour, plus more for the work surface

4 tablespoons unsalted butter, cut into 4 pieces, plus more for greasing

1 teaspoon sea salt

In a medium saucepan, cover the parsnip with fresh water. Bring to a simmer over medium heat, cover, and cook until soft, about 15 minutes. Drain. Combine the yeast and ⅓ cup of the warm milk in a measuring cup. Set aside for 10 minutes in a warm place.

Transfer the parsnip to a food processor. Add the yeast mixture and process until smooth, about 20 seconds. Let the mixture stand until bubbly, about 30 minutes. Add the remaining 1 cup warm milk and 1 cup flour. Process just until combined. Transfer to a large bowl, cover, and let rise in a warm place until doubled in volume, about 2 hours. Knock down and knead in the remaining 3¼ cups flour, butter, and salt. Knead until soft and pliant but no longer sticking to your fingers.

On a lightly floured surface, roll the dough out into a 14-inch round about ½ inch thick. Cut out biscuits with a 2½-inch round cookie cutter and arrange on two greased baking sheets. Cover with a cloth and let the biscuits rest until risen and puffy.

Preheat the oven to 375°F. Transfer the baking sheets to the oven and bake until the biscuits are golden brown on the bottom, 15 to 20 minutes.

HEIRLOOM PARSNIPS

In 1806, Philadelphia horticulturist Bernard McMahon advertised seeds for a parsnip varietal called "Long Garden." These closely resembled the parsnips known to the ancient Romans, which means that while parsnips were a critical root crop for most kitchen gardens, not much effort had been devoted over the centuries to improving them. People ate parsnips but they were more commonly used as fodder for livestock, especially milk cows. By the 1820s this coarseness had been bred out with the development of the varietal known as "Hollow Crown," now a classic and still as popular today as it was around 200 years ago.

Since parsnips thrive in heavy soil, they are often used as cover crops to break up the ground for more sensitive food plants. Our local Pennsylvania soil is rich in minerals but also rich in clay, so "The Student" is the variety we maintain at Roughwood. Its wedge-shaped root is ideal for doing a little spade work naturally, and since it was selected in 1847 from a wild parsnip in the English Cotswold Hills, its hardy origin makes it a perfect tool for soil amendment, at least in terms of texture. The Student's story is a telling example of how now-valuable heirloom produce can be created out of marginal weeds.

If you grow parsnips be aware that the sap in the stems and leaves is photo-toxic, meaning that it is activated by sunlight. The chemicals involved are furanocoumarins, whose role is to protect the plant from animals that might eat it, including us. Gardeners handling parsnip greens should wear gloves or risk breaking out with a burn-like rash worse than poison ivy: there is no cure other than to sit it out.

Nettle Tart

At Roughwood nettles appear early in the spring, their dark green shoots unfolding along the perimeter of the garden. Common stinging nettles are invasive, so we keep them contained to border beds as barriers against deer. Most people who cultivate nettle or let it grow wild in damp places along ponds and streams are familiar with the perennial species called *Urtica dioica*, which can grow quite tall. The best nettle for culinary and medical purposes, however, is Roman nettle (*Urtica pilulifera*). It is also shorter and will hold its bright green color when cooked. You can make this recipe all spring and summer, but nettle, regardless of the species, is best and most healthful when harvested before it blooms in late June or early July.

To harvest nettle, wear gloves and cut off the stems with scissors. Trim the leaves from the stems, including the small stem on each leaf. Rinse the leaves and dry thoroughly in a salad spinner. Last, put the leaves in a plastic bag and weigh the amount you need. Wearing gloves, gather the leaves into a bunch then chop coarsely with a sharp knife. Once chopped, the nettle leaves should release a sweet fragrance that will also permeate the tart. For a vegetarian version of this recipe, simply omit the slab bacon and substitute 3 tablespoons toasted walnut oil for cooking the onions, and instead of the diced bacon add ½ cup chopped walnuts to the cooked onion and nettle mixture. In the summer, when the nettles are spent, substitute the same weight of amaranth leaves.

Serves 6 to 8

1 prepared piecrust, rolled out to a 12-inch round

1 cup diced slab bacon (about 4 ounces)

3 small onions, cut in half lengthwise, then sliced paper-thin

4 ounces chopped nettle leaves (enough leaves to fill a 2-quart bowl)

3 large eggs

1¼ cups heavy cream (or 1 cup milk mixed with ¼ cup sour cream)

2 tablespoons rice flour or potato starch

Sea salt and freshly ground black pepper

Freshly grated nutmeg, to taste

Preheat the oven to 400°F. Line a 9-inch pie plate with the piecrust. Fold over and crimp along the edge to keep the filling from running over; set aside.

In a broad sauté pan, cook the diced bacon over medium heat until just lightly browned. Remove the bacon to a paper towel–lined plate, reserving the drippings in the pan. Add the onions, cover, and sweat over medium heat until soft, about 4 minutes. Add the chopped nettle leaves, cover again, and cook until the nettle has wilted and turned dark green, about another 3 minutes. If necessary, splash a little water over the leaves to create more steam and use this moisture to deglaze the pan. Add the reserved bacon and transfer the mixture into the prepared pie plate, spreading the filling evenly over the bottom and patting it smooth with a wooden spoon.

Beat the eggs until a lemon color and frothy, then whisk in the cream and rice flour until thoroughly combined. Season with salt, pepper, and nutmeg, then carefully pour the egg mixture over the nettle filling. Transfer to the oven and bake until the tart puffs and turns golden brown on top, 25 to 30 minutes. Serve hot.

Ramp Pesto

Wild-harvest ramps have become quite popular of late, but our woodlands are being stripped of these once-plentiful onions because little care is being taken to leave behind enough plants to reproduce. Pulling up the bulbs is one certain way to send this spring delicacy into extinction. However, harvesting the leaves, or a few from every other plant, will ensure that the bulbs flower and produce seeds. It can take seeds 2 to 3 years to germinate; judicious harvesting can keep a woodland patch healthy and sustainable.

This is what we practice at Roughwood, where we have a nice stand of ramps in a woodsy corner of the garden. This is also why we have developed this recipe using the leaves only. The flavors of this pesto are complex, with dill enhancing the ramps' subtleties. Its texture is thick and creamy and it freezes well! Unlike many basil pestos, that darken on exposure to the air, this one also holds its bright green color even when frozen. Cotswold cheese is a pungent, creamy Double Gloucester flavored with chives and onions and is well worth seeking out. This pesto is perfect served with Allegheny Fardel Cakes (see page 110).

Makes 2 cups

1 cup extra-virgin olive oil

4 tablespoons broken or chopped walnuts

½ teaspoon sea salt

2 garlic cloves, chopped

2 tablespoons fresh lemon juice

½ cup freshly grated Cotswold cheese

4 cups ramp leaves, coarsely chopped

1 cup chopped fresh dill

To the bowl of a food processor, add the oil, nuts, salt, and garlic and process until smooth, about 1 to 2 minutes. Add the lemon juice, cheese, ramp leaves, and dill. Process until thick and smooth, another 2 minutes, scraping down the bowl as necessary. Taste and adjust seasoning. Serve immediately or transfer to lidded airtight jelly jars. Pesto will keep in the refrigerator for about 1 week; frozen, the pesto will keep up to 1 year.

Rhubarb Conserve

My great-grandmother prepared this conserve with Strawberry Rhubarb, a rare old cultivar that seldom blooms, thus it remains good for cooking all summer and well into the fall. As its name implies, it is a classic pairing with strawberries. My grandfather pampered his row of strawberry rhubarb and fertilized it annually with well-rotted pigeon manure, a practical by-product from his huge flock of racing pigeons. It thrived and sometimes the stems were 2 inches in diameter, yet so tender you could eat it raw without the stringiness of some common varieties. If your rhubarb seems stringy when you slice it, it's worth it to pull off the strings before proceeding; otherwise, your conserve will contain annoying little threads.

Makes about 7 cups

5 cups organic sugar

3 pounds rhubarb stems, cut into small slices (see Note)

Juice of 1 lemon

8 ounces sun-dried figs, cut into thin strips

⅓ cup green raisins

Shredded zest of 1 orange

1 cup English walnuts, coarsely chopped

In a deep work bowl, combine the sugar and rhubarb with the lemon juice and let stand at least 10 hours or overnight. The rhubarb and sugar will become syrupy.

Pour the mixture into a large preserving pan and set over high heat. Stir and cook until thick, about 15 minutes, then add the figs, raisins, and orange zest. Cook another 10 minutes then stir in the walnuts.

Pour the hot conserve into sterilized jelly jars and set them in a glass dish partially filled with hot water. Carefully transfer to a microwave and heat for about 1 minute or until the conserve begins to bubble. Remove and cover with sterilized lids and rings. Turn the jars upside-down on a rack for 5 minutes then turn upright. They should self-seal within 10 minutes. You can also fill the sterilized jars then boil 10 minutes in a hot-water bath to seal.

If the jars do not self-seal, keep the conserve in the refrigerator for up to 1 week. Sealed jars will keep in a cool, dark place up to 1 year.

Parsnip-Rhubarb Soup

The complex flavor of this soup is dependent upon striking the right balance of sweet and tart, so the amount of sugar needed will be determined by the rhubarb itself. Its tartness varies from one variety to the next, so tailor the recipe to what you're growing and add the sugar little by little, to taste. Serve with Parsnip Biscuits (page 27).

Serves 4 to 6

2½ pounds parsnips

1 pound rhubarb stems

5 ounces leeks, washed, trimmed, and chopped (white parts only)

2 to 4 fresh bay leaves, to taste

2 quarts chicken stock or vegetable stock

½ cup sugar (see Note)

Sea salt

Chopped rhubarb stems, for garnish

Peel the parsnips and chop them and the rhubarb into 1-inch chunks. Transfer to a 2-quart saucepan and add the leeks, bay leaves, and stock. Bring to a simmer over medium heat, then cover and cook until the parsnips are soft and the rhubarb has completely dissolved, about 30 minutes.

Remove the bay leaves then transfer the mixture to a blender. Carefully puree until smooth and creamy, about 2 minutes. Return to the same pan over medium-low heat and rewarm until hot.

Add the sugar and salt to taste. If too thick, thin the soup with additional hot water or stock, up to 1 cup. Serve immediately with chopped rhubarb stems. You can also transfer the soup to a large bowl, cover, refrigerate and chill completely to serve cold.

Rhubarb Relish

This is a great condiment or appetizer but can also be used as an accompaniment for roasted pork, poultry, fish, or pickled meats such as souse. Its flavor is refreshing, slightly sweet-and-sour, and the bright color adds a cheery note to the spring harvest table.

Makes 3 cups

1½ pounds rhubarb stems (the redder the better, see Note, page 34)

1 cup honey

2 cups white wine vinegar

Peel the skins off the rhubarb stems and combine them in a nonreactive stewing pan with the honey, vinegar, and 2 cups spring water. Simmer about 30 minutes or until all the color is extracted from the skins; the liquid should be a vibrant, hot pink.

While the mixture is simmering, chop the peeled stems into small, bite-size pieces and transfer to a nonreactive work bowl or glass container.

Strain the liquid, discarding the skins, and pour over the rhubarb. Cover and let cool to room temperature; the rhubarb will turn a rich pink. Place in the refrigerator to chill until needed. To serve, use a slotted spoon to transfer the chopped rhubarb to a dish and add enough liquid to loosen the mixture as desired. Relish will keep in the refrigerator up to 1 week.

Stir-fried Lettuce with Spring Peas

This very lightly cooked vegan salad, if I may call it that, takes inspiration from Thai stir-fries. It elevates simple lettuce to a new level and makes excellent use of various delicious odds and ends coming out of the garden at this time of year. To work quickly, prepare all the ingredients first and arrange them on the counter or on a tray in the order called for within easy reach of the stove.

Serves 4 to 6

2 large heads Romaine lettuce

4 ounces snow peas, trimmed

¼ cup roasted peanut oil

1 small leek, washed, trimmed, and chopped (white parts only)

6 scallions, thinly sliced on the diagonal (white parts only)

1 cup peas, fresh or frozen, thawed,

3 garlic cloves, minced

¼ cup light soy sauce

3 tablespoons unseasoned rice vinegar, or to taste

½ cup coarsely chopped toasted peanuts

1½ teaspoons *gochugaru* or crushed red pepper flakes

1 teaspoon ground star anise

Trim off the tops of the lettuce leaves, leaving about 6 to 7 inches, then slice the heads crosswise into 2-inch segments and set aside in a large bowl. Pick out the smallest of the snow peas and set them aside in another bowl; cut the remaining snow peas into thin slices and add these to the whole pods.

In a wok or large, broad sauté pan, heat the oil over medium-high until just smoking. Add the leek, scallions, and snow peas. Toss until the vegetables change color, about 3 minutes. Stir in the peas and garlic. Cover, reduce heat to medium, and cook about 2 minutes, then add the chopped lettuce and stir to coat. Cover and cook another 4 minutes, then add the soy sauce, vinegar, and peanuts.

Cover and cook another 2 to 3 minutes, then remove from the heat. Stir in the gochugaru and star anise and serve immediately.

Stuffed Spinach Leaf Beets

Spinach Leaf beets are hardy perennials that ought to have a place in every well-managed kitchen garden. The leaves are large and beautifully bright green, although you can use any sort of chard for this recipe. In fact, I have made it with my grandfather's Golden Chard, which famously holds its golden-yellow color even when cooked. Regardless of the chard you choose, I strongly recommend using a white poaching stock so the leaves do not blacken when baked. This little culinary trick does not affect the flavor but definitely improves eye appeal.

Serves 8 to 10

½ cup extra-virgin olive oil

2 medium onions, coarsely chopped (about 1½ cups)

2 cups bulgur wheat, rinsed

2 packed cups chopped nettle leaves (see Note, page 30)

4 scallions, white and green parts chopped (about ½ cup)

3 garlic cloves, minced

¼ cup finely minced dill

⅓ cup finely minced flat-leaf parsley

½ cup coarsely chopped pitted kalamata or Halkidiki olives, or a mix of both

½ cup coarsely chopped walnuts

2 teaspoons whole dill seed

3 large eggs

2 tablespoons potato starch

2 teaspoons sea salt

Freshly ground black pepper, to taste

¼ cup fresh lemon juice

2 tablespoons all-purpose flour

20 whole spinach leaf beet or chard leaves, each about 9 by 6 inches, stems trimmed

6 cups Roughwood Tomato Sauce (page 89) or marinara sauce

Minced parsley and lemon thyme; chopped fresh rosemary; or toasted and chopped walnuts or almonds, as garnish

Bring about 1 quart of water to a boil in a saucepan. In a broad sauté pan, heat the oil over medium heat until just shimmering, then add the onions. Stir, cover, and cook until the onions are soft, about 5 minutes. Add the bulgur, stirring it well to coat it with oil, cover, and cook another 5 minutes, taking care not to scorch the onions. Carefully add 3 cups of the boiling water to the sauté pan, cover, and simmer over low heat until the wheat is cooked and the water has been absorbed, 15 to 20 minutes.

Stir with a fork to fluff the grains then add the chopped nettle and cover. Sweat the mixture over medium-low heat just until the nettle is wilted, about 3 minutes, then remove from the heat and set aside to cool.

Once the mixture has cooled to room temperature, add the scallions, garlic, dill, parsley, olives, walnuts, and dill seed; stir to combine.

In a small bowl, beat the eggs until a lemon color and frothy, then whisk in the potato starch. Stir into to the wheat mixture until thoroughly combined, then add the salt and season with pepper. Filling can be chilled and refrigerated overnight; return to room temperature before filling and rolling leaves.

In a large pot, heat 2 quarts of water over medium heat until just steaming. Using a measuring cup, remove ½ cup of the hot water. Add the flour and stir to make a slurry. Stir this back into the pot and add the lemon juice. Bring up to a boil for 2 minutes then reduce the heat back down to a simmer. Using tongs, gently dip the leaves one at a time into the poaching stock just until wilted, about 20 to 30 seconds at most. Then remove the leaf and spread it flat on a clean work surface or baking sheet lined with paper towels. Continue in this manner until all the leaves have been poached then gently pat them dry. Discard the poaching water and preheat the oven to 400°F.

Place a scant ⅓ cup of the stuffing mixture in the center of each leaf. Fold the sides over the stuffing, fold the bottom (stem) end upward, and finally cover this with the top part of the leaf folded downward. This will create a roll similar to a stuffed cabbage. Once rolled, pack the stuffed leaves snugly in 2 glass baking dishes or 1 large roasting pan. Pour ½ cup water around the stuffed leaves, cover tightly with foil, and bake 10 minutes, then add the tomato sauce, cover, and bake another 15 to 20 minutes, or until the sauce is bubbling. Serve immediately, garnished with chopped herbs or nuts.

Upland Cress Bisque

What to do with an abundance of Upland Cress? It reseeds promiscuously, and and if you keep a patch of it in reserve, you can harvest it all winter as a biennial. It revives toward the end of February and pushes new growth in March, so you can make good use of it until it begins to bloom in April. After that it turns bitter, so let it run to seed and move on to freshly planted garden cress (which can also be used in this recipe). Since Upland Cress grows close to the ground, you will want to wash it carefully and dry it in a salad spinner. I find the best heirloom potatoes for this soup are floury types, like Lumper or Snowflake.

Although I prefer to style it like bisque, this is truly a *potage purée*. If it resembles vibrant vichyssoise, well, that too is a good description. It is a refreshing way to grace a spring dinner, especially as a starter course, or as a mid-meal palate cleanser.

Serves 6 to 8

1½ pounds floury potatoes, scrubbed (see Note)

4 tablespoons unsalted butter, at room temperature

1 quart vegetable stock enhanced with a soup bunch (see page 193)

1 pound cress, tender stems and leaves only

8 scallions, white and green parts chopped (about 1 cup)

¼ cup all-purpose flour

½ teaspoon freshly ground white pepper

½ teaspoon freshly grated nutmeg

2 tablespoons tarragon vinegar

Sea salt, to taste

Sour cream, for serving

Chopped chives and whole cress leaves, for garnish

Preheat the oven to 450°F. Arrange the potatoes in a heavy baking pan and cover tightly with foil. Bake just until tender, 45 to 50 minutes. Immediately remove the potatoes from the roasting pan and, once cool enough to handle, peel (or halve and scoop out the potatoes); discard the jackets. Press the potato through a ricer or strainer into a large bowl and stir in the butter until combined.

In a saucepan, heat the stock over medium heat until hot. In a bowl, toss the cress and chopped scallions with the flour then stir into the hot stock and cook until the stock has thickened, about 10 minutes. Transfer to a blender and carefully process until thick and creamy, about 1 minute. For the smoothest texture, press the puree through a chinois or conical strainer to remove small fibers.

Whisk the puree with the reserved potatoes until smooth. Transfer the mixture to a large pot and season with the white pepper, nutmeg, vinegar, and salt to taste. Soup will keep in the refrigerator up to 3 days. Reheat until hot and serve with a spoonful of sour cream; garnish with chopped chives and cress leaves.

Summer

Feast of the Corn Mother

While spring on Devon Hill starts very much like spring in Yorkshire, May flies south quickly, landing squarely in the humid environs around Madrid. It happens that we are on roughly the same latitude as the Spanish capital, so summers at Roughwood transform the kitchen garden into a Mediterranean paradise. This amazing diversity is reflected in the regional cookery of southeastern Pennsylvania, which flourishes under the blazing sunlight. We receive a lot more rain than Spain, and this natural lushness is perhaps why Lenape Indians first settled here thousands of years ago, and by degrees assimilated the culture of corn from neighboring peoples to the south. Corn thrives in our climate and it defines the historic food culture of the Americas. It determined the cycles of planting and harvest, life and death, birth and rebirth. Corn was also the food of the gods. The "hands" of the Corn Mother were especially sacred—they are cobs that develop small offshoots from the main, like fingers—and were never eaten but displayed as totems.

The planting in late spring initiated this new seasonal cycle. The ancient idea of planting corn in hills migrated north from Mexico and Central America. Each hill could be the womb of Mother Earth, thus from her body sprang corn. Per some creation myths, humans were shaped from corn and their blood derived from corn. By planting corn, people were planting themselves in a place as well as propagating their spiritual mother. The Iroquois then brought the sacred trio of the Three Sisters—corn, beans, and squash, planted together. Corn-planting ceremonies varied greatly from nation to nation, provided they even grew corn, as some did not. Since the Iroquois managed to remain in their homeland while other groups were eventually expelled to the West, finalized by the Indian Removal Act of 1830, the food culture remained as well, becoming part of local lore. Contrary to some popular garden literature, the Three Sisters was not simply a practical gardening technique; it was a component of and connected to religious principles.

Even the number of plants per hill varied from one tribal group to the next. For example, among the Cherokee, seven was a sacred number, thus each corn hill contained seven plants. Among the Lenape, a sacred number was twelve, thus each hill received twelve seeds. The twelve seeds of the Lenape represented the twelve clans into which each of the three Lenape tribal groups was divided. In this sense, each plant was endowed with totemic significance as understood by the shamans who oversaw the religious needs of each community.

This brief discourse on the religiosity of corn is intended to help you better appreciate the complex meanings assigned to the Green Corn Moon, as the full moon in August was once called, and the spirituality of the food connected with it. Because the Corn Mother conflicted with western Christian ideas and European agricultural practices, as white settlers overtook the land, corn became de-spiritualized as an agricultural crop. Suppression of Native American foodways due to cultural prejudice ignored the fact that unripe green corn was not just symbolic in value, it was also used and venerated as a remedy for the sick. Who might have known that Lenape *Sehsapsing* (a variety of black flour corn) contains one of the highest percentages of anthocyanin of any corn grown today, more even than blueberries? It is an antioxidant superfood with many benefits. While we think of giving thanks at the end of the growing season, there are many reasons to express gratitude to the Corn Mother before harvest. Each step along the way from planting to harvest could be cause for celebration.

I like to imagine that we have introduced that same spiritual connectedness to the garden at Roughwood. The ebb and flow of summer harvest brings new joys and surprises as one week folds into the next. I cannot claim that the Lenape farmed on Devon Hill because it was covered with towering chestnut trees well into the nineteenth century, but in 1983 Lenape from Oklahoma did return and burned white sage and sacred tobacco and left many happy memories under our great oak tree, since it was here when their ancestors still roamed these hills. I know they are out there because on a still night, I hear the fairies rustle among the corn, and see strange little lights darting like fireflies. Thus, does the cycle of the Corn Mother continue, and from their flowery nests in the garden corners, I hear the *Eckleit* singing songs of summer.

Apple and Corn Salad

For this summer salad, use any market-fresh sweet corn, or even ears a few days old. We want kernels that will remain whole, giving our salad a loose texture. If the corn seems too raw and starchy, simply poach it in boiling water until it floats. Regarding the *coztomatl* berries, which are a fun option in this recipe, these are a rare Mexican ground cherry that grows into a tall bush and produces fruits that taste like green apples when eaten raw.

One of the other special ingredients in this salad is lovage, an herb whose flavor can be partially replicated by combining parsley and green celery leaves. If you have lovage-flavored vinegar on hand, even better— use that in place of the wine vinegar in the salad. Do not leave out the grapefruit zest. This small touch will amplify the flavor of the salad with just the right hit of acid in the dressing.

Serves 4 to 6

4 cups fresh sweet corn kernels cut from the cobs (3 to 4 ears)

½ cup chopped scallions (white and green parts), plus additional, sliced, for garnish

3 tablespoons finely minced shallot

½ cup finely diced red bell pepper

1 cup peeled and diced tart green apple or *coztomatl* berries (see Note)

⅓ cup coarsely chopped walnuts or broken walnut bits

2 tablespoons white wine vinegar

3 tablespoons roasted walnut oil

2 tablespoons minced fresh lovage (or fresh celery and parsley leaves)

1 teaspoon grated grapefruit zest

Sea salt

¼ teaspoon freshly ground black pepper, or to taste

Thinly sliced scallions, for garnish

Combine the corn kernels, scallions, shallot, bell pepper, apple (or coztomatl berries), and chopped walnuts in a deep work bowl.

In a separate work bowl, whisk together the vinegar and walnut oil until emulsified. Pour the mixture over the vegetables and stir until combined. Add the lovage and grapefruit zest, and season with salt and pepper. Cover and refrigerate for about 1 hour to let the flavors to marry.

Before serving, bring the salad to room temperature and garnish with sliced scallions.

Carrot Marmalade

There comes a time during the summer when the carrots need thinning. Too small for cooking other than as additions to stir-fries or soup stock, the culls happen to be ideal for marmalade. Their small size and tenderness are just right for this type of preserve, especially if you happen to be growing several different heirloom varieties. Combining white, yellow, and orange carrots creates a colorful mixture that ornaments the marmalade with special eye appeal, which is why I like to use it as a gift during the holidays. If you have only orange carrots, then shred them as instructed below but increase the amount to 2½ cups. Use the large holes of a vegetable shredder to create toothsome shreds. Mix the grapefruit and orange juice and segments in equal portions if sour oranges are not available. Like most marmalades, this one may take several days to fully set.

Makes 6½ cups

4 sour oranges (see Note)

2 lemons

¾ cup shredded white carrot

¾ cup shredded orange carrot (see Note)

¾ cup shredded yellow carrot

⅓ cup sugar-free pectin (or 1 package Sure-Jell)

4½ cups organic sugar

To put up the marmalade for gifting or storage, sterilize the jars and lids in boiling water before you begin. Keep hot.

Using a vegetable peeler, shave wide strips of zest from 1 sour orange and 1 lemon, Chop the zest into fine shreds with a sharp knife. Juice 1 sour orange to yield 1 cup fresh juice—using another orange as needed. Juice the lemon to yield ¼ cup fresh lemon juice (you may not need the other lemon). Peel the remaining 2 sour oranges and separate the segments. Remove any seeds with a paring knife and puree the segments in a food processor.

In a deep, nonreactive preserving pan, combine the zest, juice, orange puree, and shredded carrots over medium-low heat. Cover and cook gently until the carrots are tender, about 8 minutes. Stir in the pectin, increase the heat, and bring to a full boil for 1 minute. Add the sugar and boil another 1 minute. Once the sugar has boiled hard for 1 minute, skim off any foam that has formed, and transfer the hot marmalade to the prepared jars.

Cover each with a lid, screw it down tightly, and turn the jars upside down on a wire rack for 5 minutes. After 5 minutes, turn them upright and let them seal. Once sealed, store in a cool, dark pantry for up to 1 year. Keep any jars that don't seal in the refrigerator and use within 1 week.

Carrot Marmalade
2019

crafted for
sealed for

Chrysanthemum Melon Salad

This beautiful and highly unusual melon comes from Japan, where it is rightly a delicacy. The flavor is similar to honeydew, but sweetness will vary greatly depending on soil and growing conditions. For the best garden results, grow the melons on a trellis so that they are off the ground and exposed to ample airflow. With smooth, white, waxy skin, the fruit best suited for salad should be about 3 inches in diameter, weighing about eight ounces. The important point is that they are all the same size so that the individual serving portions are equal. Garnish with fragrant New Guinea basil or Thai basil to enhance the star anise in the dressing.

Serves 8

⅓ cup fresh lime juice

8 whole star anise pods

4 tablespoons superfine sugar

1 teaspoon grated lime zest

½ cup plain yogurt

4 large chrysanthemum melons

½ cup peeled, pitted, and chopped fresh lychees (about 16)

1 Asian pear, peeled, cored, and finely diced

Minced basil, for garnish (see Note)

In a small bowl, combine the lime juice and star anise pods. Cover and chill at least 6 hours and up to overnight to infuse. Strain out and discard the star anise. Stir in the sugar, lime zest, and yogurt until combined. Chill 30 minutes.

Use a sharp knife to trim the base of each melon so it sits flat. Halve each melon through the center and remove the seeds, leaving a hollow in both halves. Trim off the stem ends so all melon halves sit flat.

Stir together the chopped lychees and diced pear. Fill the center of each melon with the mixture, then top with a few spoonsful of the dressing. Garnish liberally with minced basil. Serve cold with grapefruit spoons so diners get some of the melon with each bite.

Cucumber Soup with Hominy

This rich and refreshing soup is perfect for a hot summer evening to go with a glass of chilled rosé or sparkling wine. While you can certainly give the soup a little boost of heat with a dash of cayenne pepper or hot sauce, it is even better when served with pepper sherry, an old-school spicy condiment originally from the Caribbean. A pepper sherry recipe using scotch bonnets may be found on page 38 of *The Roughwood Book of Pickling*.

Serves 6 to 8

2 quarts plus 1 cup vegetable stock

4 ounces sourdough bread, crust removed (weigh after trimming)

2½ pounds seedless cucumbers

2 tablespoons unsalted butter

1 cup chopped onions

½ cup chopped parsley

½ cup chopped lovage or celery leaves and parsley (see Note, page 48)

1 tablespoon sugar, or to taste

3 cups white hominy (*mote blanco*)

2 cups heavy cream

Sea salt and freshly ground black pepper

Thinly sliced cucumber, chopped chives, borage flowers, or dill, for garnish

In a small saucepan, bring 1 cup vegetable stock just to a boil. Tear the sourdough bread into small pieces and pour the hot stock over the bread in a heatproof bowl. Let the bread soak until all the liquid is absorbed, then stir vigorously with a fork until smooth. Set aside.

Peel and chop the cucumbers into small pieces. In a medium saucepan, heat the butter over medium-low heat. Add the cucumbers and onions, cover, and sweat the vegetables until soft, about 20 minutes. Stir in the 2 quarts stock, reserved bread mixture, parsley, lovage, and sugar then bring up to a boil. Lower the heat and simmer about 30 minutes. Carefully transfer to a blender and puree, in batches if necessary, until smooth, or run the mixture through a food mill or conical strainer, and return to the saucepan.

Rinse the hominy under running water and add it to the saucepan. Bring the mixture back to a gentle boil, then immediately remove it from the heat and let cool. Stir in the cream and chill until cold. Adjust seasonings and garnish with cucumber slices, chives, borage flowers, or dill.

Eggplant Caviar

The Mediterranean summers in my part of Pennsylvania allow us to grow many varieties of eggplants. Dips like this one first appear in local cookery in the nineteenth century, when the Philadelphia Style first emerged from classical French cuisine. I have served this recipe many times, because it is a perfect addition to a summer buffet. It can be served hot on toast like bruschetta or at room temperature as a cocktail spread. A hint to the host: Its flavor improves if made a day ahead.

Serves 6 to 8

2 pounds young eggplants (the fewer seeds the better)

¼ cup extra-virgin olive oil

1 cup finely chopped onions

1 cup tomato paste

3 tablespoons red wine vinegar

3 garlic cloves, minced

2 tablespoons sugar, or to taste

2 teaspoons sea salt, or to taste

1 teaspoon freshly ground white pepper

¼ teaspoon freshly grated nutmeg

¼ teaspoon cayenne pepper, optional

Crackers or flatbread, for serving

Anchovy fillets, sliced hot peppers, parsley leaves, roe, for garnish (optional)

Preheat the oven to 225°F. Cut the eggplants in half lengthwise and lay them cut side down in a baking pan. Add 1 cup water and cover the pan tightly with foil. Bake until soft, 45 to 50 minutes, then scoop the pulp from the skins and transfer to a food processor. Puree until smooth.

In a large stewing pan, heat the oil over medium-low heat. Add the onions, cover, and sweat slowly in the oil just until transparent, 4 to 5 minutes. Stir in the pureed eggplant, tomato paste, vinegar, garlic, sugar, salt, pepper, nutmeg, and optional cayenne, if you like a little heat. Cover and cook over a low heat for 10 minutes, to heat the ingredients through and blend the flavors; stir frequently to keep the paste from scorching. Remove from the heat, cool to room temperature then cover and refrigerate for up to three days. Serve at room temperature on crackers or flatbread, garnished as desired.

Fig Balsamic Vinegar

I cannot remember when I began to make this recipe for fig balsamic vinegar, but I do recall being disappointed by the bottled products sold under that name in Italy. While I'd be tempted to say it was the long list of preservatives (which must affect the taste), in truth it probably had more to do with the fruit. Figs so soft and ripe they drop right into your hand when touched—those are the right figs for balsamic vinegar. The other key to this recipe is perhaps obvious but still true: Use actual balsamic vinegar and not an imitation. Everything else in this recipe depends on the combination of fig fruitiness and balsamic acidity. You must strike a balance, which will vary season-to-season, batch-to-batch. The wine and vanilla introduce a smooth character to the vinegar, rounding out its intensity. My friends tell me that you can serve this decadent sauce on almost anything. This recipe's saving grace is that while the up-front grocery bill may seem high (mostly for the vinegar), one batch will last 2 to 3 years, so averaged out it is good economy. Come February you will be very glad to have it on hand for a taste of summer.

Makes 2½ quarts

3 pounds fresh, tree-ripened black or brown figs, stemmed

6 cups good-quality balsamic vinegar

3 cups organic sugar

Grated zest of 1 orange

½ cup dry Marsala wine, or to taste

2 or 3 fresh vanilla beans, or good-quality vanilla extract to taste

Mash the figs by hand or puree in a food processor until still slightly chunky. In a large, nonreactive preserving pan, combine the figs, vinegar, sugar, and orange zest over medium heat. Bring to a gentle boil and cook until the figs break down and the mixture thickens, about 30 minutes, stirring occasionally to prevent scorching.

Pour the thickened mixture through a strainer or colander, pressing with a wooden spoon to smooth out the texture. Transfer to a nonreactive container, cover, and let cool to room temperature. Add the wine and vanilla to taste.

Pour into sterilized canning bottles, snap down the lids, and store in a cool, dark place or in the refrigerator for up to 3 years. The vinegar will keep well at ambient temperature but preserves its best flavor when kept under refrigeration.

Garlic Scape Sauté

Garlic scapes have become the hottest thing in seed-to-table cookery, yet have been with us for as long as anyone has planted garlic. The flower heads must be removed in order for the garlics to focus on swelling out into succulent bulbs. So, what to do with the prunings? Small-scale farmers who grow garlic might admit they make more from the scapes than from the rest of the plant; no matter, if you grow your own garlic you can have it both ways. Choose very young scapes, taking care to trim off the bottoms of the stems, which can be tough. This recipe is better when made the night before and allowed to marinate. Refrigeration will cause the sauce to thicken, so reheat the mixture just enough to thin the sauce. Let it stand until room temperature and serve immediately as a vibrant starter.

Serves 4 to 6

2 tablespoons extra-virgin olive oil or duck fat

2 tablespoons dark brown sugar

8 ounces tender garlic scapes, trimmed

1½ cups chopped fresh tomatoes

¾ cup white wine

Sea salt and freshly ground black pepper, to taste

1 tablespoon chopped parsley

4 ounces halloumi cheese, grilled or seared in a hot pan

In a broad sauté pan, heat the oil over medium. Add the sugar and stir until melted, 2 to 3 minutes, then stir in the garlic scapes. Cover and cook over medium-high heat until just tender and bright green, about 3 minutes, shaking the pan from time to time to prevent scorching. Add the tomatoes and wine and stir to deglaze the pan. Cover, reduce the heat to low, and cook until the scapes are tender but not soft, another 5 to 6 minutes. Season lightly with salt and pepper (remember the cheese will be salty), then add the parsley and diced halloumi and serve at room temperature.

Green Corn Marmalade

While true green corn is intended here, freshly picked white sweet corn will work as well. At issue is the fast-changing shift to starch as corn matures, so even sweet corn will be slightly less sugary than underripe green corn. Increase up to double the amount of peppers if you enjoy spicy heat.

Makes 6½ cups

2 cups green corn or white sweet corn kernels (2 to 3 ears fresh or frozen, thawed)

½ cup grapefruit juice, plus more as needed

¾ cup finely diced red bell pepper

½ cup finely diced hot green pepper, such as jalapeño (see Note)

3 garlic cloves, minced

1 cup yellow sweet corn kernels

1 teaspoon cumin seeds

Grated zest of 1 lime

⅔ cup freshly squeezed lemon juice

⅓ cup no-sugar pectin (or 1 package Sure-Jell)

4½ cups organic sugar

To put up the marmalade for gifting or storage, sterilize jelly jars and lids in boiling water before you begin. Keep hot.

In a blender or food processor, combine the green corn kernels and grapefruit juice and puree until thick and milky. Measure out exactly 1½ cups, adding a little more grapefruit juice if needed.

Transfer the mixture to a nonreactive preserving pan and add the bell pepper, hot pepper, garlic, yellow corn kernels, cumin, lime zest, and lemon juice. Bring to a gentle boil over a medium heat and stir in the pectin until dissolved. Cook for about 3 minutes, then add the sugar. Increase the heat to high and bring the mixture to a rolling boil for exactly 1 minute. Skim off any foam that has formed and transfer the marmalade into the prepared jars.

Cover each with a lid, screw it down tightly, and turn the jars upside down on a wire rack for 5 minutes. After 5 minutes, turn them upright and let them seal. Once sealed, store in a cool, dark pantry for up to 2 years. Keep any jars that don't seal in the refrigerator and use within 1 week.

Green Corn Spoon Bread

We have been growing the rare *Avati Moroto Mita* flour corn of the Guarani tribe in Paraguay for several seasons now, and aside from its striking beauty, this is perhaps one of the most valuable heirloom corns in our Native American collection. Its name translates as "small child yellow corn," small referring to its short height in relation to other corn varieties. Naturally, our interest lies in this corn's culinary potential, and we have a summertime winner. This recipe is an adaptation of traditional Paraguayan *chipá guasú* using the *Avati Moroto Mita* corn. Any good-quality freshly picked sweet corn may be used as a substitute, but better when picked two to three days *before* it would be sold as sweet corn, which means it will be sweeter and milkier than sweet corn ready for roasting. Besides its delicious use as green corn, once *Avati Moroto Mita* is ripe and fully dry on the cob, it can be ground coarsely for grits or finely for a superior white masa harina.

Serves 6 to 10

1 tablespoon vegetable oil, for the baking dish

Masa harina, for the baking dish

2 tablespoons extra-virgin olive oil

2 medium onions, chopped

1 tablespoon *merkén* (page 73) or your preferred ground hot pepper

2 tablespoons ground coriander

6 cups green corn kernels scraped from the cob (6 to 8 ears), divided

6 large eggs

½ cup buttermilk or plain yogurt

12 ounces shredded fresh *queso Paraguayo*, or another soft, salty cheese, such as feta

Sea salt, to taste

Grease a 2-quart casserole or baking dish (preferably earthenware) and dust liberally with masa harina. Set aside. Preheat the oven to 350°F.

In a large pot, heat the olive oil over medium. Sweat the onions until soft, about 4 minutes. Transfer the onions and their cooking oil to a food processor and add the merkén, ground coriander, and 3 cups green corn kernels and puree until smooth. Pour the mixture into a deep work bowl. In a medium bowl, beat the eggs until a lemon color and frothy, then stir in the buttermilk. Fold the egg mixture into the corn puree, followed by the shredded cheese and remaining green corn kernels. Season lightly with salt (the cheese is already salty) and pour the mixture into the prepared baking dish.

Bake until a rich golden crust forms on top, about 1 hour and 20 minutes. Serve hot or at room temperature straight from the baking dish.

Green Corn Stew with Linguini

South American culinary custom requires this classic Chilean summer stew be made with shelling beans fresh from the pod. My favorite among the cranberry types is the *Sapitos* or "Little Frog Bean," which is indigenous to the region around Aconcagua and Valparaiso. Aside from their rich, nutty flavor, Sapitos shelling beans retain their unique decoration even when cooked. *Ají Blanco Cristal* is an aromatic pale white-green pepper from Peru. Its mild heat dissipates within minutes of eating, and the crunchy texture is similar to celery.

Porotos Granados con Rienda is in many ways a celebration of summer, since it also calls for freshly picked corn, tender squash from the morning's harvest, and an abundance of onion, basil, cumin, and oregano. The addition of linguini broken into short pieces is also traditional and transforms the dish into a complete one-pot meal. The local corn of choice would be the ancient Araucano, a yellow flint corn similar to Gaspé (see Note, page 159).

Serves 8 to 10

5 ears of freshly picked white sweet corn, or young flint corn in the milk stage

2 quarts vegetable stock (or equal parts vegetable and chicken stock)

¼ cup extra-virgin olive oil

1½ cups chopped onion

3 cups diced yellow summer squash

3 cups shelling beans removed from their pods

2 ounces linguini or other long dry pasta, broken into short lengths

2 teaspoons ground cumin

2 tablespoons *merkén* (page 73), or to taste

4 tablespoons minced basil

2 tablespoons minced oregano

3 cups chopped *Ají Blanco Cristal* or mild hot pepper

Over a large bowl, grate the corn from the cobs and set aside—this should yield about 4 cups of grated corn, but a little more or less is fine. Using a cleaver or sharp knife, cut the cobs in half. In a stewing pan, combine the halved cobs with the stock and 2 cups water over medium-high heat. Bring to a simmer and cook 25 to 30 minutes, then strain stock into a clean pot and and discard the cobs. This creates a rich, slightly sweet, corn stock.

In another deep pot, heat the oil over medium. Add the onions, cover, and sweat 5 minutes. Add the strained corn stock, grated corn, squash, beans, pasta, cumin, and merkén and simmer over a medium heat until the corn, squash, and beans are cooked, about 15 to 20 minutes. Once the vegetables are tender, add the basil, oregano, and chopped peppers. Continue cooking until the peppers are hot but not soft, about 5 minutes. Serve immediately.

Coztomatl Jam

The ancient Aztec *coztomatl* (*Physalis coztomatl*) is not a true ground cherry, although it looks like one. The sticky berries ripen milky green and taste like gooseberries or Granny Smith apples, so they can be used like those fruits or even rhubarb in recipes. When we decided to grow this rare Mexican heirloom at Roughwood, we had no idea that it would thrive in Pennsylvania. Its unusual flavor jumps to the fore in this recipe. This is not a sweet spread for morning toast, rather a sophisticated, spicy condiment for grilled meat, roasted pumpkin, or anything fried.

Makes 7 cups

2½ cups green (unripe) *coztomatl* berries

1 cup chopped unripe mango

¼ cup seeded and chopped hot red chile pepper

¼ cup chopped cilantro (leaves only)

2 teaspoons ground cumin

1 cup fresh grapefruit juice

¼ cup fresh lime juice

⅓ cup no-sugar pectin (or 1 package Sure-Jell)

½ tablespoon unsalted butter

4½ cups organic sugar

To put up the jam for storage, sterilize jars and lids in boiling water before you begin. Keep hot.

In a blender or food processor, combine the *coztomatl* berries, mango, red pepper, cilantro, cumin, grapefruit juice, and lime juice and puree until coarse. Transfer the mixture to a deep preserving pan and stir in the pectin and and butter. Set over high heat and bring to a rolling boil for 1 minute, then add the sugar. Boil another 1 minute then carefully transfer the hot jam into the prepared jars. Cover each with a lid, screw it down tightly, and turn the jars upside down on a wire rack for 5 minutes. After 5 minutes, turn them upright and let them seal. Once sealed, store in a cool, dark pantry for up to 1 year. Keep any jars that don't seal in the refrigerator and use within 1 week.

Hot Pepper Jam

At Roughwood, the end of summer floods the garden with an overabundance of peppers, especially the hot varieties. Jam is one way to capture their snappy garden-ripe freshness for enjoyment during the doldrums of winter. The degree of heat in this jam is entirely up to you, but I've found the flavor improves with a mix of hot and sweet peppers. Red, yellow, and green are recommended, with at least 2 habanero-type peppers to give the mixture a kick of spice and smoke. Remember that sugar can suppress the peppers' heat, so don't skimp. And lastly, this jam is delicious but slow to set: Allow 7 to 10 days. I find Certo gives the best jell for peppers; if using another pectin, you may need to adjust the amount of sugar.

Makes 7 cups

½ cup tomato paste

1 cup red wine vinegar

½ cup garlic-flavored vinegar

1⅔ cups seeded and finely diced sweet pepper (mix of red, yellow, and green)

½ cup finely diced hot green pepper (including 2 to 3 unripe habaneros)

Grated zest of 1 lime

½ cup minced cilantro (leaves only)

1 teaspoon whole cumin seeds

6½ cups organic sugar

1 (6-ounce) pouch Certo (or ⅓ cup pectin, see Note)

If putting up the jam for storage, sterilize jars and lids in boiling water before you begin. Keep hot.

In a nonreactive preserving pan, combine the tomato paste, red wine vinegar, garlic vinegar, diced sweet and hot peppers, lime zest, cilantro, and cumin over medium heat until just simmering. Add the sugar, increase the heat to high, and bring the mixture to a rolling boil for 1 minute. Stir in the pectin and boil hard another 1 minute, then take the pot off the heat.

Ladle the jam into the prepared jars. Cover each with a lid, screw it down tightly, and turn the jars upside down on a wire rack for 5 minutes. After 5 minutes, turn them upright and let them seal. Once sealed, store in a cool, dark pantry for up to 1 year. Keep any jars that don't seal in the refrigerator and use within 1 week.

Lemon Blush Pie

One of the most beautiful of all the yellow tomatoes is a rare heirloom called Lemon Blush. It is large, smooth, and lemon yellow with a rose-pink blush on the blossom end, and has a flavor that verges on tropical fruit. First developed by Elbert S. Carman at the end of the nineteenth century, the Lemon Blush was thought to have gone extinct, but we found seed in a private collection in New Jersey and are excited to see it flourish again. If you are growing Lemon Blush: Letting just-picked tomatoes finish ripening in the sun for 2 to 3 days enhances their rich, citrusy flavor. Arranging the tomatoes blossom-end up will induce the fruits to develop their distinctive pink blush, which in turn further increases their sweetness.

Its unusual flavor can be traced to one of its breeding parents, the yellow French peach tomato, *Tomate Pêche Jaune*. Most French peach tomatoes, which have fuzzy skins just like peaches, were used to make jams and jellies. That hint of fruitiness makes Lemon Blush perfect for summer pies.

Serves 8 to 10

1 prepared piecrust, rolled out to a 12-inch round

2 cups pitted, peeled, and sliced yellow peaches (from about 2 whole)

2 cups pitted and sliced underripe pluots or black plums (from 2 to 3 whole)

2 cups sliced Lemon Blush tomatoes, 1 slice reserved for garnish (from 2 to 3 whole)

⅓ cup chopped pecans, plus 10 pecan halves for garnish

1 tablespoon grated lemon zest

2 tablespoons fresh lemon juice

¾ cup sugar, or to taste, depending on sweetness of peaches and tomatoes

¼ cup potato starch

½ teaspoon freshly grated nutmeg

½ teaspoon sea salt

¼ teaspoon cinnamon

Preheat the oven to 375°F. Gently fit the piecrust into a 9-inch glass or earthenware pie plate; fold over and crimp the edge as desired.

In a deep work bowl, combine the sliced peaches, pluots or plums, tomatoes, chopped pecans, lemon zest, and lemon juice. In a separate bowl, whisk together the sugar, potato starch, nutmeg, salt, and cinnamon. With a spatula, gently fold the dry ingredients into the fruit mixture to coat.

Using a slotted spoon, fill the prepared pie shell with the fruit mixture, reserving the juices in the bowl. Lightly rearrange and smooth the surface of the fruit with a wooden spoon, but do not compact. Pour the reserved juice over the fruit to fill nearly to the top of the crust—give yourself at least ¼ inch to avoid the juices boiling over.

Top with the reserved tomato slice then arrange the pecan halves in a circle around it. Bake for 30 minutes, then reduce the temperature to 325°F and continue baking until the pie is set in the center, about another 25 minutes. Cool on a rack. Serve at room temperature or slightly chilled.

Merkén

Merkén is a smoky-spicy seasoning blend, created by the Mapuche tribe of southern Chile. It has become so popular with South American chefs it can now be found online, but it's rewarding to make your own. The Chilean *Cabro de Cacha* (Goat Horn) pepper is a member of the *Capsicum annuum* species, which means that it is related to the common bell pepper. For this reason, it is easy to grow and will produce huge yields of fruit from August until frost. The traditional process for merkén involves drying whole peppers in the sun for days until brittle. Once thoroughly dried, the peppers are then cold-smoked over wood fires. The smoked peppers get seeded and crushed into small flakes, then milled into a fine powder. The powdered pepper is then mixed with salt, ground coriander, and a small amount of ground cumin for merkén. For the adventurous, Roughwood has been growing the *Cabro de Cacha* pepper for several years and they're fun to smoke. As an alternative, use ground chipotle cut with paprika.

Makes about ¾ cup

8 tablespoons ground cold-smoked *Cabro de Cacha* pepper (see Note); or 6 tablespoons paprika mixed with 2 tablespoons ground chipotle pepper

1⅓ tablespoons fine sea salt

1 tablespoon ground coriander

2 teaspoons ground cumin

Combine the pepper or paprika–chipotle pepper mix, salt, coriander, and cumin in a small mixing bowl. Pour into a ziplock bag and seal. Store in an airtight container away from direct sunlight for up to 1 year.

Merkén Sauce

Makes 1 cup

1 large red bell pepper, seeded and chopped

⅓ cup cleaned and trimmed sliced leek (white part only)

2 teaspoons merkén (this page) or ground chipotle pepper

1 teaspoon sea salt

In a small saucepan, combine the bell pepper, leek, and merkén powder with 1 cup water over medium-high heat. Cover and bring just to a rolling boil, then remove from the heat and let stand 30 minutes for the vegetables to infuse. Transfer to a food processor or blender and puree the mixture until thick, then press it through a conical strainer or chinoise until smooth. Season with salt. This sauce can be made ahead and frozen for later use.

New Guinea Basil Pesto

New Guinea basil is perhaps one of the most unusual of all the basils we grow when it comes to flavor. Eaten raw, the palate experiences a slight sensation of menthol, a hint of pepper, and distinct back notes of star anise and fennel. The plants are also strikingly ornamental from any angle—their narrow pointed leaves are blotched with purple in the centers as well as underneath.

This is not the sort of pesto you might expect from the traditional Ligurian recipe. Its flavors are rich but subtle, and they strengthen as the pesto chills. Besides pasta and as a sauce for grilled meats, the pesto is delicious on grilled vegetables (especially sweet potatoes) and pairs surprisingly well with Asian flavors—try it as a dipping sauce for steamed dumplings or pot stickers. If you can't find sour oranges, combine equal parts fresh lime, grapefruit, and orange juices.

Makes about 3 cups

4 ounces sourdough bread, crusts trimmed off (weigh after trimming)

¼ cup sour orange juice (see Note)

4 cups New Guinea basil leaves, rinsed and spun dry

½ cup macadamia or almond oil

1 cup ground toasted macadamia nuts or almonds

1 teaspoon ground star anise

Sea salt

In a large saucepan, bring at least 2½ cups water to a boil over medium-high. Tear the bread into small pieces and transfer to a deep, heatproof work bowl. Pour 1¾ cups boiling water over the bread and let stand until the water is absorbed, about 30 minutes.

In a food processor, combine the sour orange juice, basil, and oil and puree until smooth.

Drain the soaked bread in a colander to remove any excess liquid then add to the basil mixture along with the macadamia nuts and star anise. Puree until thick and smooth. Season with salt and transfer the pesto to a bowl, cover, and refrigerate until well chilled or overnight. Bring to room temperature before serving.

Pesto—It's Not Just for Tomatoes and Mozzarella!

There is a common misconception that pesto is (just) a summery green dip made with sweet Italian basil. The truth of the matter is that what we think of as "pesto," the delicious regional Genovese specialty, happens to be only one of innumerable true pestos found in cuisines across the world. The actual culinary concept is at least medieval (possibly ancient Greek), a pesto being any type of dip or sauce produced by vigorously pulping the ingredients, traditionally in a cold marble mortar with a pestle. Essentially, pesto is a pulped sauce and most green pestos in the past were made with parsley or smallage (wild celery). This also means that, technically, Greek *skordalia* and Lebanese hummus are pestos because that is how both dishes were originally made. Refried beans could be called a cooked "pesto," since the beans were originally pulped. Knowing where to look, it is easy to find numerous and fascinating examples of pesto preparations; furthermore, the texture of a pesto pulped by hand in a mortar is much lighter and more delicate than what is pureed by a food processor.

In the Middle Ages, pestos and other sauces were intended to balance the Galenic humors of the food being served. Their purpose was more medical than culinary. Sourdough bread created a neutral base with a creamy texture. Citrus or vinegar always played a role, creating an emulsion with the oil. Sweet basil was considered warming and drying from a medieval medicinal standpoint, and thus it would be served with fish—cold and moist. Ramp pesto (page 33) exhibits the same characteristics as garlic, being warm and drying, and for this reason it matches well with "cold" foods like root vegetables or wet (boiled) foods like pasta. Many local or seasonal food pairings that we take for granted in modern cookery can be traced back to these old Galenic ideas.

Sour Pickled Plum Tomatoes

This old-fashioned 1860s Pennsylvania Dutch recipe has been a longtime favorite of mine. It was originally meant to be eaten with ham, pork chops, or other smoked meats, but it works beautifully in any situation where a robust sweet-sour flavor is called for. It even makes a great addition to baked beans. The tomato for this recipe should be a red plum variety—the two best choices are both Italian, *Rei Umberto* (King Humbert) and the intensely favored *Piennolo del Vesuvio*, which has been grown on the sides of the famous volcano for well over a century. Both tomatoes hale from around Naples, so they will thrive in the hottest part of the garden; furthermore, they are super-abundant.

Makes 8 to 12 pints

7 pounds small red plum tomatoes (see Note)

1 tablespoon shredded mace

1 tablespoon whole cloves

3 pounds light brown sugar

3 cups red wine vinegar

Bring a saucepan of water to a boil. Place the tomatoes in a large colander and pour the boiling water over them to blister the skins. Using a paring knife, peel the tomatoes but leave them whole. Arrange the peeled tomatoes in layers in a deep, nonreactive preserving kettle, scattering the mace and cloves between the layers as you proceed.

In another nonreactive saucepan, combine the sugar and vinegar over high heat. Boil hard for 5 minutes, skimming off any foam, then immediately pour the hot mixture over the tomatoes. Cover and let sit 24 hours.

The following day, transfer the mixture to a deep, nonreactive preserving pan. Bring to a boil over medium-high heat, stirring to ensure the tomatoes heat evenly. As they cook, they will shrink to resemble figs. To put up the tomatoes for storage, sterilize jars and lids in boiling water as the tomatoes heat through. Keep hot.

Reduce heat to medium and cook 5 minutes. Using a slotted spoon, lift the tomatoes from the simmering liquid and distribute them evenly among the jars. Boil the liquid for another 10 minutes, then pour it over the tomatoes and seal the jars. Bring a large pot of water to a boil and give the jars a 10-minute water bath. Carefully remove from the hot bath, let cool, and store in a dark pantry for up to 1 year

Pickled Carrots with Chipotle Peppers

If possible, try to find firm green tomatoes about the same size as a whole walnut in the shell or large strawberry. If you prefer your pickles very spicy, increase up to double the amount of chipotle peppers.

Makes 6 cups

2 pounds mixed carrots (yellow, white, and orange)

4 large garlic cloves, thinly sliced lengthwise

6 fresh bay leaves

1 medium onion, cut in half lengthwise, then sliced paper-thin

5 small green tomatoes, quartered, then halved

1 cup seeded and diced sweet red pepper

6 whole dried chipotle peppers (see Note)

½ jalapeño pepper, seeds removed, sliced crosswise (about 8 slices)

1 tablespoon whole allspice (about 50 berries)

1 teaspoon cumin seeds

4 cups white wine vinegar

¾ cup organic sugar

2 tablespoons pickling salt

To put up the pickled carrots for storage, sterilize canning jars and lids in boiling water before you begin. Keep hot.

Bring a large pot of water to a gentle boil over medium heat. Trim and peel the carrots, then cut each into 2-inch-long matchsticks. Carefully add the chopped carrots to the boiling water and let simmer gently until tender but not soft, about 2 minutes—they should be at least al dente. Drain and transfer the carrots to a large work bowl.

While the carrots are still hot, add the garlic, bay leaves, onion, green tomatoes, red pepper, chipotle peppers, jalapeno, allspice, and cumin and stir until combined. Pack the mixture into the prepared jars and keep warm.

In a nonreactive preserving pan, combine the vinegar, 1 cup spring water, sugar, and pickling salt and bring to a rolling boil over medium-high heat. Boil 2 minutes then pour over the carrot mixture. Top with the lids and screw down tightly. Turn the jars upside down on a rack or clean work surface and let stand 5 minutes then turn upright to seal. The lids should pop downward within a few minutes. Keep any unsealed jars in the refrigerator for up to 1 week.

Let the pickle infuse for 1 month for the flavors to develop before opening. This pickle will keep at ambient temperatures for up to 1 year.

Pickled Daylily Buds

Daylily buds make a delightful pickle, especially if you harvest a variety of shapes (some buds are even round). The best choices are the large flowering hybrids known among lily experts as "full-form" since their buds are much larger than common ditch lilies and come in a wide variety of shapes. The trick is to get them while still green, four or five days before they enlarge to open. Daylily seedpods can also be pickled like okra if harvested before the seeds form inside.

Lily buds have a natural almond-honey aroma, which is greatly accentuated when honey vinegar is used in the pickling brine. Honey vinegar is mead that has turned to vinegar and can be found online—it is a much-underutilized vinegar with many health benefits; I make my own at Roughwood. Brining will normally turn green buds yellow, so do not be alarmed by this color change. Due to the shape of the buds and texture of this pickle mixture, I recommend using square one-pint canning jars. This shape will also reduce shrinkage because the buds will lose as much as a quarter of their volume.

Makes 8 cups

1 pound daylily buds with stems

3 small onions, cut in half lengthwise, then sliced paper-thin

8 fresh bay leaves

1 teaspoon whole allspice berries (about 24)

1 tablespoon whole coriander seeds

1 tablespoon yellow mustard seeds

1½ cups honey vinegar (see Note) or white wine vinegar

¾ cup organic sugar

2 tablespoons pickling salt

To put up the pickled daylilies for storage, sterilize 1-pint square canning jars and lids in boiling water before you begin. Keep hot.

In a deep work bowl, combine the daylily buds and onions. Distribute the bay leaves, allspice, coriander, and mustard seeds evenly among the prepared jars. Pack the daylily mixture into the jars and set in a pan of hot water.

In a nonreactive preserving pan, combine the vinegar with 3 cups spring water, sugar, and salt and bring to a full boil over high heat. Immediately pour the hot mixture into the prepared jars to cover.

Top with the lids and screw on tightly. Turn the jars upside down on a rack or clean work surface and let stand 5 minutes then turn upright to seal. The lids should pop downwards within a few minutes. Once sealed, let cool, and store in a cool, dark pantry for up to 6 months. Keep any unsealed jars in the refrigerator for up to 1 month.

Pickled Spaghetti Peppers

Word has it among pepper aficionados that this unusual specimen was first created in a greenhouse in Sweden, which is an ironically cold origin for scarlet peppers nine inches long, or longer, and full of heat. Their unique shape and ample yield ready these peppers for all sorts of culinary fun, not the least being that they pickle very well, whether green or red (ripe). They also make flavorful garnishes and colorful additions to salads.

This pepper grows on a compact bush, so you can plant it in a pot or tub on your terrace. The bushes are so ornamental that you almost hate to spoil them by harvesting the pods, but do so anyway. I find using square one-pint canning jars will best keep the peppers from migrating to the top once the brine is added.

Makes 1 quart

15 whole ripe spaghetti peppers

4 fresh bay leaves

2 large cloves garlic, thinly sliced lengthwise

1 tablespoon yellow mustard seeds

10 whole allspice berries

1½ cups organic sugar

1½ cups shallot vinegar

2 teaspoons pickling salt

To put up the pickled peppers for storage, sterilize 2 one-pint square canning jars and lids in boiling water before you begin. Keep hot.

Cut each pepper in half lengthwise and remove the stem, seeds, and veins. With a sharp knife, slice the pods lengthwise as thinly as possible, into long strips. Transfer the sliced peppers to a deep work bowl and add the bay leaves, garlic, mustard seeds, and allspice. Pack the pepper mixture tightly into the prepared jars.

In a nonreactive preserving pan, combine the sugar, vinegar, and salt and bring the mixture to a rolling boil over high heat. Immediately pour the hot brine over the peppers. Seal with the prepared lids and rings and turn the jars upside down on a rack or clean work surface for 5 minutes, then turn upright to cool. The lids should pop downward after a few minutes, indicating the seal. Sealed jars will keep in a cool dark cupboard for up to 3 years. Keep any unsealed jars in the refrigerator for up to 1 week.

Pumpkin Dumplings in Squash Blossom Miso

This is one of my favorite summer soups because it is so light and easy to eat. Once you make it you will have an all-new appreciation for squash blossoms. Choose the largest blossoms for flavoring the stock, especially from winter pumpkins (*Cucurbita maxima*) or squash from the *moschata* species, whose flowers exhibit the same melon-like sweetness as the fruit. Savory kombu, an edible dried kelp, contains naturally occurring glutamates that act as a flavor amplifier for the stock. Organic miso stock can also be found in specialty supermarkets or online.

Sserves 4 to 6

Squash Blossom Miso:

½ cup miso

1 medium onion, quartered

8 strips kombu, about 2 inches long

½ cup Chinese Shaoxing cooking wine

½ cup low-sodium soy sauce

About 30 fresh squash blossoms

Pumpkin Dumplings:

1 pound peeled, seeded Japanese summer squash

1 tablespoon low sodium soy sauce

1 tablespoon peeled, grated fresh ginger

1 teaspoon toasted sesame oil, plus more for the steamer

6 tablespoons panko

1 large egg, well beaten

¼ cup rice flour or potato starch

Thinly sliced scallions, for garnish

Squash blossoms, for garnish

Prepare the squash blossom miso. In a deep stewing pan, bring 2 quarts water almost to a boil over medium heat. In a small bowl, whisk miso with about ½ cup hot water from the pot until smooth. Return the mixture to the pot and stir until combined. Return to a gentle simmer (do not bring to a full boil) and add the onion, kombu, wine, and soy sauce; simmer gently until the flavors meld, about 25 minutes. Reduce the heat to medium-low, add the squash blossoms, and poach until fragrant, about 15 minutes. Once the stock is well flavored, strain out into a saucepan and discard the solids. Keep hot.

To prepare the dumplings, bring 2 inches of water just to a simmer in a large pot over medium-high heat. Ready a vegetable steamer or set a fine-mesh strainer inside the pot. Add the squash, cover, and steam until soft, about 20 minutes. Transfer to a food processor and puree until smooth. In a deep work bowl, combine the pureed squash with the soy sauce, ginger, sesame oil, panko, and beaten egg and stir to combine. Stir in the rice flour and set aside to let the batter thicken, about 30 minutes.

Return the pot to a simmer, adding more water as needed. Grease the vegetable steamer with sesame oil and add heaping tablespoons of the dumpling batter evenly spaced about ½ inch apart—you should have 16 to 18 dumplings. Cover and steam until the centers of the dumplings are fully set when tested with a toothpick, about 20 minutes.

To serve, divide dumplings among soup bowls and add enough hot miso to cover. Garnish with sliced scallions and 1 or 2 squash blossoms. Serve immediately.

Roughwood Tomato Sauce

Once the seed collection was reestablished at Roughwood in 1979, my grandmother would spend weekends here helping me test recipes, especially those I brought back from Italy. Together, the two of us developed this sauce over the years and it became a standard in the Roughwood pantry. A tomato coulis is nothing more than skinned and seeded tomatoes cooked down until thick. We have made it this time with the classic House Tomatoes from the Republic of Georgia and pink Phuket Egg tomatoes (see page 99). This combination of red and pink tomatoes changes the chemistry of the coulis, amplifying the fruitiness of the House Tomatoes. The miniature red tomatoes are intensely flavored and have been developed for small containers, including pots on balconies or even windowsills. They are also used as stuffing in famous Georgian Khachapuri breads.

Lovage is critical to the flavor profile of Roughwood sauce. If you cannot find lovage, combine equal parts celery leaves and parsley.

Makes 6 cups

2 pounds red tomatoes (see Note)

2 pounds pink tomatoes (see Note)

2 tablespoons unsalted butter

2 tablespoons extra-virgin olive oil

3 tablespoons coarsely chopped pine nuts

2 medium onions, coarsely chopped

6 large shallots, coarsely chopped

3 garlic cloves, chopped

2 tablespoons all-purpose flour

6 fresh bay leaves

1 teaspoon dried *rigani* (Greek oregano) or dried thyme

½ cup chopped lovage leaves (see Note)

2 teaspoons sea salt

1 teaspoon freshly grated nutmeg

½ cup dry Marsala

In a deep stewing pan, combine the red and pink tomatoes—whole or chopped—over medium heat. Cook just until soft. Press them through a sieve, strainer, or food mill to remove the skins and seeds. Return to the pan over medium heat and reduce the coulis to 2½ quarts; set aside.

In another deep stewing pan, heat the butter and oil over medium-high. Add the pine nuts, onions, shallots, and garlic and sweat for 2 minutes. Dust with the flour and stir to coat all the vegetables evenly. Cover and cook until lightly browned, about 3 minutes, being careful not to let the vegetables scorch. Stir in the reserved tomato coulis, bay leaves, rigani, lovage, salt, nutmeg, and Marsala. Bring just to a boil, then reduce heat to medium-low and simmer, uncovered, until the sauce has reduced by one-third, 1½ to 2 hours. Press through a chinois or conical strainer. Use immediately or let cool and freeze up to 2 years in an airtight container.

Shallots Sautéed with Dried Figs

One of the great pleasures of early summer is lifting the garlic and shallots from last fall's planting. I find the best shallot for general culinary use is French Gray: it's large, intensely flavored, and holds together well when cooked. It originated in Central Asia and was introduced into France during the nineteenth century, where it quickly became a favorite among Parisian chefs.

The strain we grow came to us from Darrell Merrell (1939–2008), known in Tulsa, Oklahoma as the Tomato Man. He was a colorful figure who inspired many to take up heirloom vegetable gardening. Darrell's passion, aside from heirloom tomatoes, was alliums, including garlic and rare onions. He had a way of finding things no one else could, so we were thrilled to add this culinary treasure to Roughwood's collection.

Serves 6 to 8

2 pounds whole peeled shallots, trimmed

6 tablespoons unsalted butter

2 tablespoons extra-virgin olive oil

⅔ cup finely chopped dried figs

8 fresh bay leaves

2 cups Madeira

1 tablespoon minced fresh rosemary

1 tablespoon minced fresh parsley

½ cup pine nuts, lightly toasted

Sea salt and freshly ground black pepper, to taste

Cut the largest shallots in half or quarters so all are approximately the same size. In a broad, heavy sauté pan, melt the butter and oil over low heat. Add the shallots and cook gently until light golden brown, shaking the pan frequently, about 10 minutes. Add the chopped figs, bay leaves, and Madeira. Cover and simmer gently until the shallots are caramelized, about 40 minutes.

With a slotted spoon, transfer to a shallow serving dish, reserving the liquid in the pan. Add the rosemary, parsley, and pine nuts to the shallots and stir to combine. Return the pan to the heat and bring the liquid back to a boil. Cook the liquid until reduced to a glaze, about 5 minutes. Adjust seasonings and pour over the shallots. Serve at room temperature.

Snake Gourd Curry

Snake gourds grow well in my part of Pennsylvania so long as they are planted early in May. Being tropical, they want a long growing season and hot summer evenings. The frilly white flowers attract unusual moths, while the leaves, which smell like burnt rubber, will deter deer—indeed, some plant the gourds along fences to create an effective deer barrier. For cooking, harvest the young green gourd before it ripens into bright orange and be certain to remove the seeds: they are toxic. Tailor the amount of hot pepper to your taste and depending on the spiciness of the curry powder. If growing gourds is not your thing, you can probably find snake gourds at local Asian or Indian markets, and possibly even as a frozen vegetable.

Serves 4 to 6

¼ cup toasted sesame oil

1 cup diced eggplant

2 cups chopped onions

1 pound snake gourd, seeds removed, sliced into ¼-inch-thick rings

3 cups chopped fresh or canned tomatoes

1 cup seeded and diced sweet red pepper

¼ cup sugar

2 tablespoons Madras curry powder

½ cup toasted unsalted peanuts

1 teaspoon toasted fennel seeds

1 teaspoon sea salt, or to taste

Minced hot red pepper, to taste (optional)

In a broad sauté pan, heat the oil over medium-high heat. Add the eggplant and brown it lightly on all sides. Remove with a slotted spoon to a plate and set aside. Add the onions and lower the heat to medium. Cover and sweat just until soft, about 3 minutes, then add the browned eggplant, sliced snake gourd, tomatoes, sweet pepper, sugar, and curry powder. Depending on the juiciness of the tomatoes, add up to ¾ cup hot water if the mixture seems dry. Cover and cook until the snake gourd is tender, 8 to 10 minutes. Off the heat, stir in the peanuts, fennel seeds, salt, and minced red pepper, if using. Serve hot over rice or potatoes.

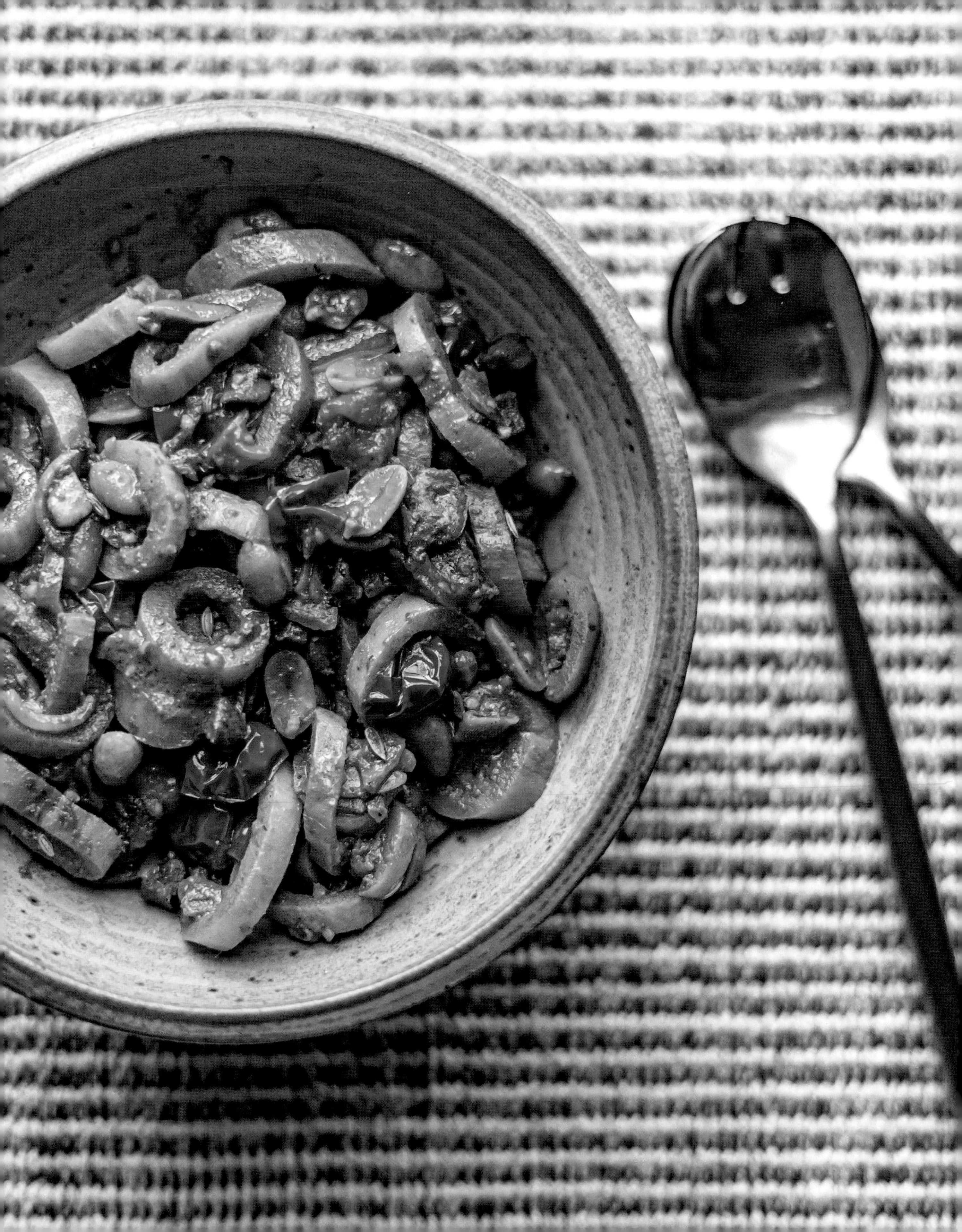

Squash *Kievé*

A dish from the indigenous Guarani peoples of the Rio de la Plata region in South America was the inspiration behind this recipe. *Kievé* means "red" in the Guarani language, referring to the color of the Andai squash used to make it, and is also the name of the dish. Its texture is a cross between mashed potatoes and polenta, with the distinctive flavors of the squash, corn, and cheese. That classic simplicity means it's also versatile on the table, from a side dish to grilled meats, a vegetarian main course served with stewed tomatoes, or even transformed into a dessert by beating eggs and sugar into it and baking it like pumpkin pudding. Furthermore, it offers a new way to deal with garden-ripe pumpkins as well as those kept over the winter, since they may have accumulated melon-like flavors during storage.

Traditional semisweet, creamy Andai squash can be challenging to find in North American supermarkets. Its rich, orange-red flesh is fragrant like cantaloupe, not surprising since it belongs to the species *Cucurbita moschata*, known for its musky flavors. At Roughwood, we grow a close approximation in the *Giraumon du Martinique*, a fragrant squash often added to spicy Caribbean pepperpots. Other comparable substitutes would be Japanese Yokohama or Kabocha squash, or an Italian butternut called Rogosa Violina "Gioia." Common butternuts can turn out disappointingly bland and flavorless; but, if they are your only option, replace half the amount in the recipe with sweet potato, especially a richly flavored variety like Red Wine Velvet.

Serves 6 to 8

3 cups vegetable stock, chicken stock, or water

¼ cup light brown sugar

2 teaspoons sea salt

2 pounds peeled and seeded squash, diced small

1 cup extra-virgin olive oil

2 cups masa harina or precooked white cornmeal

6 ounces *queso Paraguayo*, or another fresh, salty cheese such as *queso panela* or Greek feta, shredded

Sea salt and freshly ground black pepper

In a large saucepan, combine 2 cups stock, sugar, and salt over medium-high heat. Bring just to a rolling boil, then reduce the heat to medium. Add the squash, cover, and cook until tender, 20 to 25 minutes.

With a slotted spoon, transfer the cooked squash to a food processor or blender. Carefully pour in the hot cooking liquid plus the remaining 1 cup stock and puree until smooth. Transfer the mixture back to the saucepan and return to medium heat. Cook, stirring, just until hot then whisk in the oil and masa harina. Cook until thick, about 6 to 8 minutes, adding a little more water or stock if the mixture seems too thick. Stir the cheese into the squash until melted and thoroughly combined, then remove from the heat. With a whisk, whip the hot mixture until very smooth and lightened in color. Adjust seasonings and serve immediately.

Wild Muskmelon Chutney

Wild muskmelons are one of the most underutilized of all the melon varieties, yet they are among the most adaptable in the kitchen. We have planted the rare *arkopeponia* (wild muskmelon) from Cyprus for several years but similar melons can be found in many parts of eastern Turkey, Iran, Pakistan, and northern India. They are sometimes sold in Indian markets under the name *kachari* (or *kachri*). They belong to the subspecies *agrestis* and come in many different shapes, sizes, and colors.

For chutney, choose young fruit resembling baby cucumbers. Discard any large melons with well-developed seeds: they will be insipid when cooked and probably a bit tough. Young melons are tender and should cut like soft butter when sliced. They are delicious eaten raw, perfect in pickles, or served as cooked vegetables. In chutney they are classic.

Makes 4 to 5 cups

1 pound underripe wild muskmelons

8 hot green chiles, stemmed, cut in half lengthwise, and seeded

2 medium onions, cut in half lengthwise, then sliced paper-thin

3 garlic cloves, minced

2 tablespoons ground coriander

¼ teaspoon ground turmeric

2 tablespoons sesame oil

2 teaspoons cumin seeds

2 teaspoons whole coriander seeds, lightly crushed

1 teaspoon yellow mustard seeds

1 teaspoon black cardamom seeds (removed from the green pods)

2 tablespoons tamarind paste

2 tablespoons light brown sugar

½ cup chopped roasted unsalted pistachios

1 teaspoon sea salt, or to taste

Cut the melons in half lengthwise then slice evenly crosswise—slices give the chutney a more consistently chunky texture than chopped melon. In a deep work bowl, combine the melon with the green chiles, onions, garlic, coriander, and turmeric, and mix well.

In a deep, heavy stewing pot, heat the sesame oil over a medium-high heat. Once crackling hot, add the cumin, crushed coriander and mustard and cardamom seeds. Toast the spices until they begin to pop, then add the melon mixture and reduce the heat to medium-low. Stir in ½ cup warm water, cover, and sweat the melons until they turn bright green and tender, about 10 minutes. In a small bowl, dissolve the tamarind paste and brown sugar in ½ cup warm water; add to the pot. Continue cooking until most of the liquid has cooked out, another 5 to 6 minutes. Add the pistachios and adjust seasoning.

Remove from the heat and let cool. Serve at room temperature. The chutney is best when made fresh but will keep up to 1 month in the refrigerator.

Sunflower Soup (Summer Pepperpot)

The oldest known handwritten recipe for Philadelphia Pepperpot Soup dates from 1767 and, quite surprisingly, it contains sunflowers. The small, unopened buds of sunflowers were once highly prized for their nutty flavor. While historic recipes often relied on turtle as the main ingredient, here I have used duck instead—a far easier to find (and nonendangered) protein, with a similar strong flavor. We make homemade duck stock by boiling half a duck in 1 gallon water, reducing it to 3 quarts and shredding the breast and leg meat. Use whatever stock and meat you prefer: a pepperpot should reflect your personal tastes. Baby artichoke hearts, thawed if frozen or drained if jarred, have a similar nutty-green flavor and may be easier to find if you're not harvesting sunflower buds from your garden.

As to the fish pepper, which supplies the spicy heat for this soup, my grandfather acquired seeds from folk painter Horace Pippin. Years ago, I shared seed with members of Seed Savers Exchange, so the pepper is now commonly available online. For this recipe, use the fish pepper while it is still white with green stripes, before it ripens red. Its special flavor is a perfect match for shellfish, and is a classic condiment for pepperpot. If you cannot find or grow fish pepper, try serrano for similar heat. Adding shrimp may seem like gilding the lily, but it's traditional to the recipe's Caribbean roots. The soup is delicious without it, but some would say it's no pepperpot.

Serves 6 to 8

4 tablespoons unsalted butter or vegetable oil

1½ cups chopped onions

1½ cups stemmed and sliced baby okra

1 cup green cowpea pods, cut into 1-inch segments

1 cup shelled pigeon peas or green shelling beans

2 tablespoons finely diced fish pepper or serrano (see Note)

2 cups chopped cooked chicken or duck

3 quarts chicken or duck broth

2 cups diced Roma tomatoes

2 teaspoons dried summer savory

½ teaspoon freshly grated nutmeg

2 tablespoons sugar

3 tablespoons Madeira, or to taste

8 ounces small sunflower buds or baby artichoke hearts, trimmed and quartered

1 pound cooked, shelled medium shrimp, optional

½ lime

Sea salt

Chopped fresh basil, for garnish

In a deep stewing pot, heat the butter over medium heat. Add the onions, cover, and sweat just until softened, about 3 minutes, then add the okra, cowpea pods, pigeon peas, fish pepper, and chicken and stir to combine. Cover and cook until all the vegetables are hot, 4 to 5 minutes. Add the broth, tomatoes, summer savory, nutmeg, and sugar. Bring to a gentle boil, skimming off any foam, and add the Madeira, sunflowers, and shrimp, if using. Simmer just until everything is heated through. Squeeze the lime half over the soup and season with salt. Serve hot directly from the pot or as a stew over rice, topped with chopped basil.

Thai-Style Pink Tomato Jam

For this recipe we recommend the Phuket Egg Tomato, also known by its German name, *Ei von Phuket*, because a German tourist brought it into general circulation after vacationing in Thailand. The tomato ripens from white-green to raspberry-red and its chemistry is slightly different from other tomatoes. When it is combined with red tomatoes in sauce, its rich fruity character enhances the flavor of the tomatoes cooked with it, making it ideal for jams and preserves. Any well-flavored pink tomato will work in its place. Small, pointed Asian hot peppers are the type you will want (seeds removed)—Fairy Horns from Roughwood work perfectly (see page 201). Use equal amounts of lemon and orange zest if you can't find sour oranges.

Makes 6½ cups

3 pounds pink paste tomatoes, chopped

1 bunch Thai or New Guinea basil (about 1½ ounces)

6 whole star anise pods

1½ teaspoons grated lime zest

¼ cup fresh lime juice

¾ cup seeded and finely chopped hot green peppers

2 tablespoons grated sour orange zest

⅓ cup no-sugar pectin (or 1 package Sure-Jell)

4½ cups organic sugar

In a deep preserving pan, bring the chopped tomatoes to a boil over medium heat. Reduce the heat to low and simmer until the fruit is thoroughly cooked, about 10 minutes. Run the cooked tomatoes through a colander or food mill to remove seeds and skins. Measure 3½ cups puree (you may have a little leftover and can cook it down to reduce further, for more intense flavor, if desired).

While the puree is still warm, add the basil and star anise. Cover and let infuse until it reaches room temperature and is perfumed with the scent of the basil, about 30 minutes. To put up the jam for storage, sterilize jars and lids in boiling water while the puree infuses. Keep hot.

Strain the puree into a clean preserving pan over medium heat, discarding the spent basil and star anise. Add the lime zest, lime juice, green pepper, orange zest, and pectin. Bring to a rolling boil and boil hard for exactly 1 minute, then add the sugar. Bring the mixture to a rolling boil for exactly 1 minute, then immediately remove from the heat and pour into the prepared jars.

Seal tightly with the prepared lids and turn the jars upside down for 5 minutes, then turn upright to cool. The lids should pop downward after a few minutes, indicating the seal. This jam may take up to 10 days to set but will keep in a cool, dark cupboard for up to 1 year. Keep any unsealed jars in the refrigerator for up to 1 week.

Xochipilli Tamales

Any discussion of the Corn Mother eventually comes around to Xochipilli, one of the most colorful and endearing of all the ancient Aztec gods. He was a younger version of the sun god, also god of arts and crafts, song, and flowers. His festival, full of revelry, dancing, and drinking, honored the coming of summer, especially growing corn and blooming flowers. The Mexican Michoacán tradition of rolling tamales in fresh cornhusks can be used with the leaves as well, similar to the way banana leaves are used for steaming and grilling. Especially on heirloom corn varieties, the best leaves come from mid-stalk—these are the broadest and longest leaves and their tender tip-ends make for superior tamale wrappers. You can also roll the filling in traditional dried and soaked corn husks if you prefer. Non-vegetarians can substitute 2 cups of shredded cooked turkey or chicken for the chopped pistachios.

Keep in mind that the number five was sacred to Xochipilli, so if you can, serve the tamales in groups of five to keep his karma happy. We developed this recipe to brighten summer parties. You can go over the top with the garnish, as all flowers were sacred to Xochipilli.

Makes 10 to 12 tamales (depending on size of corn leaves)

6 dried guajillo peppers, stemmed and seeded

2 garlic cloves

1 cup coarsely ground masa harina, plus up to ½ cup more as needed

2 teaspoons sea salt, or to taste

1 cup dried black beans, picked over and rinsed

1 cup chopped cilantro leaves

6 crushed, seeded, and finely ground *Aji Charapita Rojo* peppers or 2 teaspoons ground habanero pepper, or to taste

2 tablespoons honey

Grated zest of 1 lime

1½ cups chopped unsalted pistachios

15 to 18 fresh corn leaves, each at least 2 feet long (you must use fresh leaves)

2 cups vegetable stock

Edible flowers, including marigolds, dahlias, cosmos, and zinnias, for garnish

Before you begin, in a large pot bring at least 2 quarts of water to a boil over medium-high heat. Adjust heat to maintain at least a simmer while making the rest of the recipe.

In a medium, heatproof bowl, cover the peppers with 2 cups hot water from the pot. Cover and let sit 30 minutes to soften then strain out the peppers, reserving the soaking liquid. Transfer the softened peppers to a blender or food processor along with ½ cup of the soaking liquid and the garlic. Puree until smooth and thick. Strain the remaining 1½ cups soaking liquid into a separate saucepan and return to a boil over medium-high heat.

Place 1 cup masa harina into a heatproof work bowl, then cover with the hot soaking liquid and stir. Add the pureed pepper mixture and stir to combine. Rinse the blender with 2 cups hot water from the pot and add that to the bowl. Whisk the mixture until smooth then transfer to a saucepan. Cook over medium heat until thick, about 20 minutes, whisking frequently to smooth out any lumps. Season with salt and set aside to cool.

While the masa harina mixture cools, place the black beans in a small work bowl and cover with boiling water from the pot. Let sit until the beans have swollen and absorbed most of the water, 30 to 40 minutes. Strain off any remaining liquid and transfer the beans to a small saucepan. Cover with hot water from the pot and bring to a simmer over medium heat. Cook until the beans are tender, 25 to 30 minutes, depending on the variety. Strain and set aside.

In a large bowl, combine the cooled masa harina mixture, beans, cilantro, ground peppers, honey, lime zest, and chopped pistachios. If the mixture seems too loose, add up to ½ cup additional masa harina until it forms a stiff paste. Adjust seasoning. This should yield about about 2½ to 3 cups of filling.

Rinse the corn leaves and pat dry. From the pointed tip end, measure 24 inches and trim off any excess. To fill the tamales, place the filling about 3 inches from the base or trimmed end of 1 leaf and spread flat. Fold the base end up over the filling and fold the sides inward. With a paring knife, just nick the leaf rib on each side of the filling to allow the leaf to fold. Continue rolling toward the tip end to form a neat package and tuck the tip into the folds. Continue with the remaining filling. Using kitchen shears or scissors, cut the unrolled leaves into long strips, about ½ inch wide. Tie 1 strip around each package, as you would with kitchen twine, to secure the tamales.

In a deep pot with a lid, bring the vegetable stock to a gentle simmer over medium heat. Set the tamales on a steamer rack or colander and lower into the pot. Cover and steam until most of the liquid has evaporated, 10 to 15 minutes. The filling should feel firm, like a dumpling. Gently lift the tamales out of the pot and transfer to a serving dish. Serve hot or at room temperature, garnished with edible flowers.

Yellow Mole

The tomatillo that we are using is the ancient *Tomatillo Amarillo de Malinalco*, a variety with a notably heart-shaped yellow fruit that was known to the Aztecs. Its flavor is similar to underripe papaya, with none of the musky funk of common tomatillos. The recipe calls for nutty, smoky cascabel peppers, which have a mild heat. When fully grown, the peppers are about the same size and shape as sleigh bells, hence the name, and turn red-brown when ripe. Pasilla chiles will also work for this mole.

Makes 2 quarts

3 tablespoons toasted sesame oil

3 medium onions

10 garlic cloves, chopped

3½ pounds yellow tomatillos, husked

8 large, fresh cascabel peppers, seeded and chopped

1 cup toasted unsalted peanuts, plus more as needed

½ cup masa harina or precooked white cornmeal

1 cup fresh Mexican tarragon leaves (*Tagetes lucida*) or ½ cup French tarragon leaves

1 cup chopped parsley

2 cups chicken stock

Sea salt

In a deep stewing pan, heat the oil over medium. Chop ½ onion, reserving the other half for another use; quarter the remaining 2 onions and reserve. Add the chopped onion and 4 chopped garlic cloves to the pan and stir to coat. Cover and sweat until soft, about 5 minutes. Using a slotted spoon, transfer the softened vegetables to a bowl and set aside.

Return the pan to medium-low heat and add the tomatillos, quartered onions, remaining 6 cloves chopped garlic, and chopped peppers. Cover and cook over medium-low until the vegetables are completely soft, 25 to 30 minutes.

While the vegetables are cooking, grind the peanuts to yield about 1¾ cups (grinding more nuts as needed). Combine the ground peanuts with the masa harina and set aside.

Using a slotted spoon, transfer the softened vegetables to a food processor or blender, add the *Tagetes lucida* and parsley, and puree until smooth. Transfer to a clean saucepan. Stir in the masa harina mixture, stock, and salt to taste. Cook over low heat just until the mole thickens.

Use the mole as a sauce over grilled chicken, turkey, or squab, and finish with toasted pumpkin seeds. You can also stew meat in the mole. Optional finishes and garnishes include toasted pumpkin seeds or sunflower seeds, calendula petals, or Tagetes lucida flowers.

Fall

Saffron Moon

Among the Pennsylvania Dutch, the Harvest Moon might more commonly be called the "Saffron Moon," because it normally coincides with the blooming of local saffron. Almost like clockwork, our saffron beds explode with color around the tenth of October and fill the garden with the rich scent of honey. This is usually during the height of our "Indian Summer," when the weather is sunny and mild with a moody fall haze, and roadside farm stands are loaded to overflowing with the season's harvest. September through October also marks the peak harvest at Roughwood and there is often not enough room to accommodate all the produce that accumulates in the kitchen. That includes an amazing crop of chicken of the woods, a fall mushroom that limb by limb has slowly consumed one of the ancient ash trees on the property. I cook them Pennsylvania Dutch–style in rich stock flavored with saffron.

In short, this section of the book is devoted to biodiversity and my own personal exploration of new food plants and their autumnal culinary possibilities. While I thoroughly enjoy reconstructing the traditional fall dishes from our region, classics like Allegheny fardel and Appoquinimink cakes, I also relish the challenge of new tastes from far-off places. What can be more transportive than an African dish made with bright green refried beans, or six-thousand-year-old chapalote popcorn from Mexico, or sorghum chapatis made with flour sorghum from Mongolia?

It is also the season when the summer's green corn has ripened, now capable of yielding a cornucopia of different cornmeals for celebrating the Corn Mother in yet another of her many personifications. Our Wandering Spirits, created by crossing several rare varieties, is not only one of the most visually beautiful flour corns now available from our larder, it honors the corn's Native American origins and tradition. We have some of those spirits in our garden, and Xochipilli, Aztec god of flowers, may be amused that we have transformed the crunchy tubers of his sacred dahlia into pickles. Like the other pickles and chutneys in this section, food from the gods is like money in the bank.

Allegheny Fardel Cake

Fardel is highland Gaelic for "a fourth of a *bannock*," that is, a round flat cake divided into quarters. In pre-Christian times, these quarters represented the four quarters of the year and thus played a role in prognostications dealing with the weather, harvest, or wished-for outcomes. The Gaelic fardel was made with oatmeal or wheat, and once they became part of the Scottish diet, potatoes were added. To follow this recipe, choose a floury heirloom potato, such as Red Cup, Snowdrop, White Peach Blow, or White Duke of York (see page 162). Besides Ramp Pesto, Fardel cakes can be spread with butter and jam like toast, smothered with gravy like biscuits or waffles, or simply sprinkled with coarse salt.

Makes 16

1½ pounds floury potatoes (see Note)

8 tablespoons unsalted butter, at room temperature

1 cup masa harina or precooked white cornmeal

1½ cups oat flour, plus more for the work surface

1 tablespoon baking powder

2 teaspoons sea salt

Ramp Pesto (page 33)

Peel and thickly slice the potatoes. Transfer to a large saucepan and cover with water. Set over medium-high heat and boil until tender and easily mashed, 15 to 20 minutes. Drain and mash well or process the potatoes through a ricer into a deep work bowl. Whisk in the butter until combined then cool to room temperature.

Sift or whisk together the masa harina, oat flour, baking powder, and salt. Using a spatula or wooden spoon, mix the dry ingredients into the cooled mashed potatoes, kneading lightly until the dough is soft and pliant. Cover and chill for 30 minutes.

Turn out the chilled dough and divide into quarters. Using your hands, shape each quarter into a ball. Lightly dust a work surface with oat flour and roll out the dough into an 8-inch round, about ¼ inch thick. With a sharp knife, divide each round into quarters. Cover with a clean towel after each round is quartered.

Heat a cast-iron skillet or heavy griddle over high heat. Once smoking hot, lower the heat to medium and add the Fardel cake quarters. Cook until browned, 3 to 4 minutes on each side. Serve hot with pesto.

Appoquinimink Biscuits

When the air turns nippy in the fall, I enjoy rifling through my recipe collection for old-fashioned specialties that evoke the early days of the Lamb Tavern—which is what Roughwood was called before the Civil War. Since we grow many heirloom grains, and grind some for flour, it seems appropriate to carry on some of the baking traditions for which the tavern was famous. One of those, beaten biscuits (see page 115), were first introduced to this region during the 1600s by the Dutch. It is true that the more you beat them the flakier they become, and while I have added baking powder to the recipe here (mainly to ensure that the biscuits come out tender), you can omit the baking powder if you beat them correctly. Real beaten biscuits do not puff when baked; rather, the authentic article should be flaky, like a piecrust.

This recipe adapts Mary Randolph's Appoquinimink Cake, named after a notable Quaker meetinghouse, from her 1824 *The Virginia House-Wife.* Try these biscuits alongside Saffron Corn Soup (page 140) or with Parsnip Curd (page 26), Rhubarb Conserve (page 34), or Carrot Marmalade (page 50).

Makes about 2 dozen biscuits

2 teaspoons sea salt

1 tablespoon baking powder

4 cups whole wheat pastry flour, plus more for the work surface

8 tablespoons unsalted butter, diced and chilled

1 large egg

⅓ cup whole milk, plus additional as needed

Preheat the oven to 425°F. In a deep work bowl, sift or whisk the salt, baking powder, and flour until thoroughly combined. Using your fingers, rub the cold butter into the flour until the mixture resembles fine crumbs or sand, with some larger pieces of butter remaining. Alternately, transfer the dry ingredients to a food processor, add the butter, and pulse until combined.

Form a well in the center of the mixture. In a small bowl, beat the egg until a lemon color and frothy, then add the milk. Pour the mixture into the center of the well and work into the dry ingredients to form a stiff paste. If the mixture is too dry and crumbles apart, add more milk, a little at a time, just until the dough holds together. Too much moisture will toughen the biscuits.

Turn the dough out onto a lightly floured work surface. Knead gently just into a ball then beat the dough with a rolling pin until soft and spongy and the dough snaps when pulled, 10 to 15 minutes. Fold and roll the dough about 5 times to make certain it is perfectly smooth on the upper and lower surfaces.

Once smooth, roll the dough out to a ½-inch thickness. With a fluted biscuit cutter, cut out 2-inch rounds and prick with a skewer, fork, or biscuit dock. Bake 15 to 20 minutes, or until lightly golden on the bottoms. Cool on racks and serve immediately or store in an airtight container for up to 3 months.

BEATEN BISCUITS

Beaten biscuits are a form of ship biscuits, the earliest versions of which were made locally by the Dutch during the 1600s at New Castle, Delaware, to provision ships returning to the Netherlands. The Dutch even built windmills to grind the wheat. Once Philadelphia was established in the 1680s, biscuit production moved north, and a detailed recipe was published by John Beale Bordley in 1799. His meticulous directions leave no doubt that "beaten biscuits" are a local variation on the original maritime version.

Ship biscuits (also called "water biscuits") were valued for their long-term keeping qualities since they were not made with butter, milk, or eggs. Along with corn pone, this type of bare-bones biscuit originally served the rural poor of the Delaware and Chesapeake Bay region as a substitute for bread and as a thickener for stews and chowders. It is also lasting evidence of how dependent the early settlers of this region were on basic commodities derived from abroad.

The earliest recipe for Maryland beaten biscuits as we now know them was published in *The Virginia House-Wife* in 1824 under the name Appoquinimink Cake (see page 112). The well-established Quaker social network that extended across the region helped popularize beaten biscuits beyond Delmarva, not surprising since Quaker Tea at that time was an important form of hospitality. Quaker Tea was very similar to English High Tea in that it resembled a buffet meal served at "early candlelight," or dusk. Many biscuit recipes steadfastly call for an iron implement to do the beating, which today we know to be inadvisable. If nothing else, iron will impart a "rusty nail" flavor to the dough. Biscuit brakes—utensils designed to beat dough—were generally made of wood, oak, or sweet gum. Reflecting their ship-borne origins, the most basic or rustic recipes for beaten biscuits (at least those eaten by poor folk) were made cheaply with lard and water; soon, special-occasion biscuit recipes emerged for high tea at genteel tables. These "parlor" biscuits were made with butter, milk, and eggs.

Buckwheat Nut Cake

We plant a lot of buckwheat as a cover crop on fallow garden beds at Roughwood, so with all we harvest in the fall, there is always an abundance of seeds. In that vein, here is a culinary journey into old Polish manor house cookery. The recipe comes from the Polish side of my family, as they served it at Krasne Potockie, a beautiful old house (now gone) with a spectacular view of the mountains. Its rich, nutty flavor makes it an ideal coffeecake, yet it is not overly sweet. Don't forget: Polish sour cream is thicker and richer than American sour cream.

Serves 8 to 10

Breadcrumbs, for the tart pan

1 cup spelt or barley flour

1 cup buckwheat flour

2 tablespoons baking powder

1 teaspoon sea salt

2 tablespoons ground coriander

¾ cup sugar

1 cup cooked buckwheat groats
(follow the instructions on the package)

1 cup plus 4 tablespoons chopped toasted hazelnuts

2 large eggs, yolks and whites separated

1 cup sour cream or *śmietana* (Polish sour cream)

4 tablespoons unsalted butter, melted

2 tablespoons coarse sugar

Preheat the oven to 375°F. Grease a 12-inch tart pan with a removable bottom with baking spray and dust it liberally with breadcrumbs.

In a deep work bowl, sift or whisk together the spelt flour, buckwheat flour, baking powder, salt, coriander, and sugar. Add the cooked groats and 1 cup chopped hazelnuts and mix until combined. In a small bowl, beat the egg yolks until a lemon color and frothy, then add the sour cream. Fold the egg mixture into the dry ingredients. Add the melted butter and stir until combined.

Using a hand mixer or whisk, beat the egg whites until they form stiff peaks. Gently fold the beaten whites into the batter until combined. Spread the batter evenly in the prepared tart pan. Sprinkle the remaining 4 tablespoons chopped hazelnuts and sugar over the top. Bake until done in the center, 25 to 30 minutes. Cool on a rack. Serve at room temperature.

Chapalote Popcorn Roast

About six thousand years old, beautiful honey-brown Mexican *Chapalote* is my favorite heirloom corn in the Roughwood Seed Collection. In fact, it is the ancestor of all corn grown today, so cooking with it is not only an adventure in original corn flavor, it is a celebration of indigenous culture. It is also the original finger food—the cobs are small, at most five inches long, and you can pop the corn right on the cob. A fragrant spice powder gives this easy snack sophisticated flavor plus a little heat.

If you don't grow *Chapalote*, you can substitute any small popcorn variety. Cherokee popcorn (available online) makes an excellent substitute. This is also a great snack (and activity) for camping. To pop the corn over hot coals, put the cobs directly onto the cleaned grill grate, turning the cobs frequently with tongs until mostly popped. Then brush with toasted walnut oil and dust with spice powder.

Serves 6 to 8

1 tablespoon fine sea salt

3 tablespoons ground coriander

1 tablespoon ground cumin

1 tablespoon ground chipotle pepper

1 tablespoon ground annatto

1 tablespoon superfine sugar

1 tablespoon garlic powder

1 tablespoon dried Greek oregano

1 teaspoon ground allspice

20 to 25 ears *Chapalote* or a similar variety of small-cobbed popcorn

Toasted walnut oil, for brushing

In a small bowl, combine the salt, coriander, cumin, chipotle, annatto, sugar, garlic powder, oregano, and allspice. The spice powder will keep several months in a jar, so you can make it ahead.

In a microwave-safe bowl, cook 4 to 5 ears at a time (do not crowd ears in bowl) on the popcorn setting until most of the kernels have burst, no longer than 2 minutes. The kernels should stay on the cob. Repeat with the other ears, brush with toasted walnut oil, then dust with spice powder and serve.

Chicken of the Woods Mushroom Soup

Chicken of the woods (*Laetiporus sulphureus*) is a showy golden-yellow mushroom that grows on trees. It commonly appears in the fall, especially during the warm days and cool, damp nights of October. For best results, chicken of the woods should be harvested when very fresh and young, that is, when still soft and tender and not touched by frost. The flavor of this local delicacy is unique with a slight hint of sweet bay when fresh, and a smoky flavor when cooked. This Pennsylvania Dutch stew is also popular as gravy over waffles (see page 167).

Serves 4 to 6

4 tablespoons unsalted butter

1 cup finely minced onion

1½ pounds chicken of the woods mushrooms, trimmed, cleaned, and rinsed

4 tablespoons all-purpose flour

1 quart chicken or vegetable stock enhanced with a soup bunch (see page 193)

6 bay leaves, bruised

⅓ cup angel hair egg noodles broken into 2-inch lengths

⅛ teaspoon powdered saffron

½ teaspoon freshly grated nutmeg

Sea salt and freshly ground black pepper

¼ cup heavy cream or sour cream, optional

In a large stewing pan, heat the butter over medium heat and add the onion. Dice or chop the mushrooms into small, bite-size pieces, then add this to the pan and stir to combine. Cover, and sweat till the onions and mushrooms have softened, about 10 minutes. Stir in the flour to coat then add the stock, bay leaves, and noodles. Bring to a simmer and cook until the mushrooms are tender and the stock has thickened, about 20 minutes. At the end of cooking, add the saffron and nutmeg and season. Off the heat, stir in cream, if using.

Kashmiri Collard Chutney

The rich, spicy flavor of this chutney comes from its blend of collards, toasted peanuts, hot chiles, and spices. I think the secret is in the collards—a rare variety from Kashmir that we have been growing for more than twenty years. Called *karam saag* (or *haak*), this delicate cool-weather green is popular throughout northern India for its spinach-like tenderness—you can even eat it raw. This is definitely a fall vegetable because it thrives under the brisk autumn sun and will produce a handsome yield of greens between first frost and the heavy snows of winter. If you do not garden, you can replicate *karam saag* by mixing equal parts freshly picked tender, young collards and spinach.

Tamarind concentrate (also sold as paste) as well as chana *dal*, spicy fried split chickpeas, and *masala moong dal*, spicy fried split mung beans, can be found in Indian markets or online.

Serves 4 to 6

6 ounces *karam saag* collard greens

2 tablespoons sesame oil, ideally organic cold-pressed

1 teaspoon black mustard seeds

1 teaspoon whole cumin seeds

10 hot green Punjabi chiles, stemmed, halved, and seeded

½ cup diced tomatoes

½ cup unsalted roasted peanuts

1 tablespoon tamarind concentrate dissolved in 2 tablespoons water

Sea salt

Chana dal or *masala moong dal* (see Note), for garnish

To prepare the collard greens, trim off the stems and remove the central vein, leaving only the tender leaves. Chop the leaves and measure out 4 cups (about 4 ounces). In a heavy stewing pan, bring 3 cups water to a rolling boil over medium-high heat. Once the water is boiling hard, reduce heat to medium, add the chopped collard greens, and simmer until soft and dark green, about 3 minutes. Drain and set greens aside, reserving 1 cup of the cooking water. Wipe out the pan.

In the same pan, heat the oil over medium-high heat until just smoking. Add the mustard and cumin seeds, stir, and toast the spices in the hot oil just until they begin to pop, 2 to 3 minutes, then reduce the heat to medium and add the chopped chiles and tomatoes. Cover and sweat 4 minutes then stir in the collard greens and ½ cup of the reserved cooking water. Cover and sweat the vegetables until the greens are hot, another 3 minutes.

Transfer the mixture to a blender or food processor and add the peanuts, tamarind infusion, and the remaining ½ cup reserved cooking water. Puree until the mixture is a smooth, green paste resembling pesto. Adjust seasoning with salt and serve over rice garnished with *chana dal* or *masala moong dal*.

Peanut-Onion Chutney

Roughwood has grown peanuts for years. They were once common in southeastern Pennsylvania, at least until World War II, after which they faded in favor of other, more profitable crops. We grow a variety of black peanuts from North Carolina (the skins are black) and they are hugely prolific. You can also find them in Central and South America as *cacahuete negros*. Growing your own peanuts also yields plant tops that make excellent compost and shells, perfect for mulching around other plants in the garden. In short, peanuts pay their own way in a kitchen garden.

Once you've tried it, the idea of making peanut butter can become anti-climactic. One of the easiest and most versatile uses for a bumper crop of peanuts is this chutney, which can also be thought of as peanut butter taken to another level. This kind of chutney is often served at breakfast in southern India, yet its winning spiciness recommends it as an accompaniment for many kinds of dishes. Not least, it is entirely vegan, and the asafoetida adds depth to the toasted spices.

Serves 4 to 6

¼ cup plus 4 teaspoons unrefined organic sesame oil

2 cups chopped onions

3 garlic cloves, finely minced

1 tablespoon ground cumin

2 teaspoons cayenne pepper or more to taste

1 teaspoon ground asafoetida

1 cup chopped toasted unsalted peanuts

⅓ cup tomato paste

Sea salt

½ teaspoon black mustard seeds

½ teaspoon whole cumin seeds

In a medium sauté pan, heat ¼ cup oil over medium-high. Add the chopped onions and garlic, lower heat to medium, cover, and sweat until the onions are soft, 3 to 4 minutes. Add the cumin, cayenne, asafoetida, chopped peanuts, and tomato paste, and stir well to combine. Cover and cook until heated through, another 3 minutes. Remove from the heat and let cool. Transfer the cooled mixture to a food processor or blender and puree to a thick paste. Season chutney with salt then transfer to a serving bowl.

In a clean sauté pan or small saucepan, heat the remaining 4 teaspoons oil until just starting to smoke. Add the mustard and cumin and toast until the seeds begin to sizzle and pop. Immediately drizzle the hot oil and seeds over the chutney and serve immediately as a condiment over rice or with naan. While its flavor is best fresh, the chutney will keep in the refrigerator up to 3 days.

Narragansett Succotash

This rich recipe is like a New England clambake rolled into succotash, a perfect late autumn tableau featuring ingredients associated with the New England coast. It also features Rhode Island White Flint Corn, supposedly given to the original Pilgrims by the Narragansett Indians; Corn Planter Yellow Pole bean, a Seneca bean also found throughout much of the Eastern Woodlands; and the Narragansett Succotash bean, which the Narragansett Indians claim as a traditional variety. Like limas, the Succotash Bean originated in South America and belongs to a class of beans known as "chestnut beans," due to their texture and flavor. As an assimilated ingredient, they make a wonderfully meaty addition to any succotash recipe; however, Succotash beans should be cooked separately because their color leaches into the cooking water. The beans change from inky black to walnut brown once cooked.

Serves 6 to 8

1 cup dried whole Rhode Island White Flint Corn kernels

1 cup dried Succotash pole beans

¾ cup dried Corn Planter Yellow pole beans

½ cup chopped scallions (white and green parts)

30 canned smoked mussels or 30 small smoked oysters

4 ounces cooked clams (about 70 small)

2 tablespoons sliced hot red pepper, or to taste

2 tablespoons minced parsley

4 tablespoons unsalted butter

2 tablespoons all-purpose flour

2 cups clam juice

½ cup heavy cream

Sea salt

Prepare the corn the day before you plan to serve the succotash. In a deep stewing pan, pour boiling water over the dried corn kernels to cover. Let stand 1 hour, then set over medium heat and simmer until the corn softens, about 45 minutes, adding more water if necessary. Remove from the heat, cover, and let the pot stand overnight with the cooking water; the corn will continue to swell. The next day, reheat over medium and continue cooking until the corn is puffed and tender, about 50 minutes. This slow cooking method will ensure that the texture resembles cooked beans. Drain and set aside.

In separate work bowls (see Note), cover the dried beans with boiling water and let stand 1 hour. Drain and transfer to separate saucepans. Cover both with fresh unsalted water and set over medium heat. Bring to a gentle boil and cook until both beans are tender, 30 to 35 minutes. The Succotash beans should double in size while the Corn Planter Yellow will stay smaller. Drain the beans and set aside to cool.

In a work bowl, combine the cooled beans with the reserved cooked corn, chopped scallions, smoked mussels, clams, hot pepper, and parsley. Transfer to a stewing pan. In a separate pan, heat the butter over medium heat. Stir in the flour until well combined and cook until beginning to turn light golden, about 2 minutes. Whisk in the clam juice until smooth then pour the mixture over the vegetables. Set the pan over medium heat and cook just until heated through and the flavors have blended. Add the cream and stir until hot, but do not boil. Adjust seasoning and serve hot.

Pickled Dahlias

Let me dispel one popular myth right now: dahlias are a food plant. The ancient Aztecs grew them as a root vegetable. That most of us grow them as flowers evolved purely by historical accident—understandably, given their ornamental beauty and variety. A practical point to consider for this application is that dahlias contain a high percentage of starch, despite their watery texture. When pickled, this natural starch leeches into the brine, turning it white, then precipitates like powder. So, when you serve pickled dahlias, shake each piece in the brine first to refresh. Besides this innocent if slightly disconcerting feature, dahlias make an excellent pickle or soup vegetable because they hold their crisp texture when cooked and do not turn mushy—try our Ginger Crunch, see page 201.

Makes 1 quart

1½ cups tarragon vinegar or white wine vinegar

1 cup mirin

¼ cup organic sugar

1 tablespoon sea salt or preserving salt

1 pound dahlia tubers, peeled and sliced

1 small onion, halved and sliced paper-thin (or ½ medium onion)

4 fresh bay leaves, bruised

8 whole allspice berries

2 tablespoons minced jalapeño or hot pepper

1 ounce fresh ginger root, peeled and thinly sliced

1 tablespoon whole coriander seeds

To put up the pickled dahlias for storage, sterilize a 1-quart canning jar and lid (or preferred size) in boiling water before you begin.

In a nonreactive preserving pan, heat the vinegar, mirin, sugar, and salt over medium-high. Bring to a full rolling boil.

In a work bowl, combine the dahlia tubers, onion, bay leaves, allspice, jalapeño, ginger, and coriander and stir to mix thoroughly; pack into the prepared jar (or distribute mixture evenly among jars).

Pour the hot brine over the mixture then seal with the prepared lid. Screw down tightly and turn the jars upside down on a rack or work surface for 5 minutes then turn upright and let cool. The lid should pop downward after a few minutes, indicating the seal.

Store at least 10 days for flavors to infuse, but the pickle is best after 6 months. Sealed jars will keep in a cool, dark cupboard for up to 1 year. Transfer any unsealed jars to the refrigerator and store for up to 2 months.

Pickled Green Jujubes

I have two jujube trees at Roughwood, and every year they produce an abundance of fruit. This profusion generally coincides with the blooming of my saffron in early October. After a few more weeks, the small green fruit will have ripened into wrinkly brown, resembling dates in taste, texture, and appearance. The challenge always seems to be what to do with them. Ripe, they make an interesting sticky addition to pies and confections; but the unripened green fruit is also edible. Since their flavor resembles green apples, unripe jujubes can be stewed and pickled with great success. This sweet and sour recipe makes an ideal condiment reminiscent of pickled crab apples though I find their texture superior. These go especially well with grilled lamb or smoked sausages.

When filling the canning jar or jars, one easy way to keep the contents hot while preparing the syrup is to stand them in a wide bowl or roasting pan and add enough hot water to the pan to come partway up the jars. This should be enough to keep your pickle from cooling down too quickly.

Makes 1 quart

3 cups organic sugar

1 tablespoon sea salt or kosher salt

1 cup garlic vinegar or white wine vinegar

6 whole star anise pods

1 pound green jujubes, stems removed

In a deep preserving pan, combine the sugar, salt, vinegar, star anise, and ½ cup spring water over medium heat and bring to a full rolling boil. Add the jujubes and cook at a steady boil until the fruit softens and turns pale yellow, about 20 minutes. Remove from the heat, cover, and let stand at room temperature until the fruit absorbs the syrup, about 12 hours.

Sterilize canning jar or jars, lid(s), and rings(s) in boiling water; keep hot. Strain out the fruit and star anise from the preserving pan, reserving the liquid, and transfer to the prepared jar or jars. Set the preserving pan with the reserved syrup back over medium-high heat and bring back to a full rolling boil. Pour the boiling syrup over the fruit then seal with the prepared lid(s). Screw down tightly then turn the jar upside-down for 5 minutes. At the end of 5 minutes, turn it right side up. As the jar cools, the lid should pop downward, indicating the seal. Store in a cool, dark cupboard up to 2 years. Keep unsealed jars in the refrigerator for up to 1 week.

Pipián of Pumpkin Seeds and Baby Peanuts

The name of this recipe may be unfamiliar. In its broadest sense, a *pipián* is a thick sauce, yet in practice more like a stew treated as a sauce. It is traditionally made with meat and even lard, but you can make a vegan version by simply eliminating the turkey and using vegetable stock. You can serve this as a one-pot meal in a bowl or as a topping over rice or even as a filling for tortillas. It is also excellent as a stuffing in peppers, especially Spanish *piquillo dulce* grilling peppers.

Alongside the mammoth *maiz de Jala*, which is famous all over Mexico, perhaps the unsung culinary wonder from the magical Jala Valley is its Miniature Peanut (*Cacahuatillo de Jala*). This rare heirloom has the most intensely nutty flavor of any we have tasted, and from a culinary standpoint, its small size can be a bonus. When used whole, it can assume the character of a small nut or pea and is not as intrusive as common commercial peanuts from a visual or textural standpoint. Furthermore, it naturally tastes sweeter than the big, starchy ones. I prefer 365 by Whole Foods Market organic fire-roasted frozen corn, which is reliably organic and is available year-round; off-season fresh corn isn't worth using.

Serves 6 to 8

For the turkey and stock:

1½-pound turkey leg (1 large drumstick or whole thigh)

1 medium onion, quartered

2 garlic cloves, sliced lengthwise into 8 pieces

4 fresh bay leaves

1 teaspoon whole cumin seeds

1 tablespoon chopped fresh oregano

For the *pipián*:

4 ounces sourdough bread, crusts removed, and roughly torn (weigh after trimming)

3 dried guajillo chiles, stemmed, seeded, and chopped or torn

½ cup extra-virgin olive oil

1 cup untoasted *cacahuetillos* or peanuts chopped in half

1 cup raw pumpkin seeds

1 cup chopped onion

1 cup frozen fire-roasted yellow corn, thawed (see Note)

2 tablespoons chopped fresh oregano

2 garlic cloves, minced

2 teaspoons ground cumin

2 teaspoons freshly ground black pepper

Sea salt

In a deep stewing pan, cover the turkey leg, onion, garlic, bay leaves, and cumin with 1 quart water. Set over medium-high heat and bring to a simmer, then cover, reduce heat to medium, and stew until the meat is tender and falling from the bone, about 1 to 1½ hours. Off the heat, add the oregano and let cool. Strain the stock into a bowl and return it to the pan. Pick out the meat and cut or shred it into bite-size pieces. Reserve meat but discard the other solids.

In a deep, heatproof work bowl, combine the torn sourdough bread and dried chiles. Return the reserved stock to a rolling boil over high heat. Carefully pour the boiling stock over the bread and chiles, cover, and let soak until very soft, about 30 minutes. Transfer the mixture to a blender or food processor. Add ¼ cup olive oil and carefully puree the hot mixture until smooth; set aside.

In a deep stewing pan, heat the remaining ¼ cup olive oil over medium-high heat. When the oil begins to crackle, add the *cacahuetillos* and pumpkin seeds. Fry until lightly toasted, 5 to 6 minutes. Add the onion, cover, and sweat until the onion is translucent, another 3 to 4 minutes. Reduce heat to medium and add the corn, oregano, garlic, cumin, black pepper, and the reserved puree. Cook until thick, about 10 minutes, and add the reserved meat. If the sauce seems too thick, add a little water to loosen. Once heated through, season with salt and serve immediately.

Pippin's Golden Honey Catsup

This delicious pumpkin-colored catsup derives its unique character from two essential ingredients, Pippin's Golden Honey Pepper, which ripens to a vibrant golden orange, and the *coztomatl*, a Mexican ground cherry with purple husks, similar to tomatillos, and a pale green fruit that has the tart flavor of Granny Smith apples. The pepper, named after folk painter Horace Pippin, is spicy and fragrant yet completely free of heat. While the flavor is unique you can substitute orange bell peppers. *Coztomatl* may be hard to find and can be substituted with an equal amount of pureed Granny Smith apples. An unexpected bonus from the *coztomatl* is that you can use them in any recipe calling for fresh green gooseberries, even where gooseberries are impossible to grow. The plant is a unique species unto itself (*Physalis coztomatl*) and is pest-free, which means low maintenance for organic gardens.

Makes 10 cups

2½ pounds ripe yellow tomatoes, chopped

2 pounds Pippin's Golden Honey Pepper, stemmed, seeded, and chopped

14 ounces coztomatl berries, papery husks removed, pureed (about 1½ cups)

1¼ cups honey vinegar (see page 81) or white wine vinegar

2 tablespoons extra-virgin olive oil

1 medium onion, chopped

2 tablespoons chopped garlic

3 tablespoons pickling salt

1 tablespoon ground coriander

2 teaspoons ground ginger

1 teaspoon freshly ground white pepper, or to taste

Honey, to taste, optional

In a deep preserving pan, cook the chopped tomatoes over medium heat just until softened, about 10 minutes. Run through a food mill or sieve to remove the skins and seeds. Return the tomato pulp to the pan over medium and cook until reduced to 4 cups, if needed. Add the peppers, cover, and cook until the peppers are very tender, about 30 minutes. Remove from the heat, stir in the coztomatl puree and honey vinegar, and set aside.

In a small sauté pan, heat the olive oil over medium heat. Add the onions and garlic. Cover and sweat 2 to 3 minutes, then stir into the reserved pepper and tomato mixture. If putting up the catsup for storage, sterilize bottles and lids or jars, lids, and rings in boiling water; keep hot.

Transfer to a food processor or blender and puree until thick and creamy. Using a spatula, push the puree through a conical strainer or chinoise to remove any remaining pepper skins. Pour the strained puree into a clean saucepan and add the salt, coriander, ginger, and white pepper. Set over medium heat and bring to a simmer. Cook, stirring, until the mixture thickens, about 10 minutes. Adjust the seasoning with additional pepper or honey, if you prefer a little sweetness.

Pour the catsup into the prepared bottles or jars. Bring a large pot of water to a rolling boil and seal closed bottles in a 15-minute water bath. The catsup will keep, stored in cool, dark place, up to 3 years.

Peruvian Pepperpot (*Soppa de Aji Amarillo*)

This spicy Peruvian soup uses *aji amarillo* for both flavor and heat. The challenge here is to add depth without overpowering the natural fruitiness of the peppers. This delicate balance is achieved with fresh lime juice, a minimum of sugar, and a generous portion of salt. Add a little of each at a time until just right. For cooks unfamiliar with the golden *aji amarillo* pepper, it is one of the cornerstones of Peruvian cuisine, handed down from the Incas. It has no equal for green banana-like flavor, except perhaps for its big brother, the *aji lengua de perro* (Dog's Tongue Pepper), which is twice the *amarillo* size and ripens pumpkin orange. Its complex flavor once fully ripe can even suggest mango. Use what you have on hand for this dish, including rotisserie chicken from the market or leftovers from a roast dinner. *Huacatay* is an Andean herb related to marigolds; it's easy to grow and is becoming more common in markets.

Serves 6 to 8

6 to 8 *aji amarillo* or 4 *aji lengua de perro* peppers, seeded and chopped

1 pound tomatoes, skinned, seeded, and chopped

1 medium onion, chopped

3 garlic cloves, sliced

10 cups chicken or turkey stock

2 cups peeled and diced potato

1½ cups diced cooked chicken or turkey

1½ tablespoons diced sweet red pepper

2 tablespoons fresh lime juice

1 teaspoon shredded sour orange zest, or equal amounts of lemon and orange zest if you can't find sour oranges

2 teaspoons sugar, or to taste

Sea salt

Chopped *huacatay*, for garnish (optional)

In a large stewing pan, combine the peppers, chopped tomatoes, onion, garlic, and stock over medium heat. Bring to a simmer and cook until the vegetables are soft, 25 to 30 minutes. Transfer the entire mixture to a food processor or blender and puree carefully until smooth and free of lumps. Return to the pan and add the diced potato, chicken, and red pepper. Cook over medium-high heat until the potatoes are tender, another 10 to 15 minutes. Stir in the lime juice, sour orange zest, sugar, and salt. Adjust seasoning and serve immediately, garnished with huacatay, if using.

Red Cabbage with Quince and Dried Cherries

Many years ago, I published a Pennsylvania Dutch Christmas recipe for red cabbage and quince from the Lotz family of Bethlehem, Pennsylvania. It has always remained one of my favorite wintertime dishes, in part because its festive flavors improve when reheated the next day. Using that classic heirloom recipe as inspiration, this is one of many variations. Happily, this recipe can be transformed into a one-pot meal with the addition of smoked duck breast, grilled sausages, or finely shredded prosciutto di Parma scattered over the top. If quinces are not readily available, substitute tart apples tossed with a few drops of vanilla extract.

Serves 4 to 6

1 tablespoon duck fat or extra-virgin olive oil

1 large red onion, cut in half lengthwise, then sliced paper-thin

6 cups finely shredded red cabbage

1 large celeriac

2 to 3 large quince

½ cup pitted dried sour cherries

¼ cup raspberry vinegar or red wine vinegar

3 tablespoons honey

1 teaspoon sea salt, or to taste

In a large sauté pan or wok, heat the duck fat over medium-high. Add the onion, cover, and sweat just until transparent, about 3 minutes, then add the cabbage and stir to coat. Cover, reduce the heat to a gentle simmer, and cook without lifting the lid for 30 minutes. This steaming is important for the dish's flavor and texture.

While the cabbage cooks, peel and core the celeriac. Shred against the large holes on a vegetable grater to yield 1½ cups. Repeat with the quince, discarding cores, to yield 3 cups of shreds in total. Combine in a work bowl and cover with a damp paper towel until needed to prevent browning.

When the cabbage has steamed, stir in the shredded celeriac and quince, cherries, vinegar, honey, and salt. Cover and cook, stirring occasionally to prevent scorching, until tender, 20 to 25 minutes. Serve hot as a side dish or let cool and serve at room temperature as a salad.

Quince and Celeriac Conserve

Toasted mustard seeds add a nutty flavor to this delicate autumn condiment. You will discover that this conserve is perfect with Thanksgiving turkey or roast meats in general. Its distinctive honey-like flavor comes from the quince, which should be ripe and fragrant. *Muchi* is a spicy curry blend from western India; use Madras (a more common, less spicy blend from southeastern India) or your favorite hot curry if you cannot find it.

Makes 6 cups

1 tablespoon black mustard seeds

3 cups peeled and shredded celeriac

3 cups peeled, cored, and shredded quince (from 4 to 5 large)

1 medium onion, cut in half lengthwise, then sliced paper-thin

½ cup golden raisins

½ cup unsalted pistachios, shelled and toasted

1½ cups organic unrefined cane sugar

1½ cups honey vinegar (see Note, page 81)

1 tablespoon sea salt

¼ cup cider vinegar

1½ tablespoons Muchi curry (see Note)

To put up the conserve for storage, sterilize jars, lids, and rings in boiling water before you begin. Keep hot.

In a dry skillet, toast the mustard seeds over high heat, shaking the pan constantly, until the seeds start to pop, 2 to 3 minutes. Transfer to a small bowl and let cool. In a deep, nonreactive preserving pan, combine the shredded celeriac, quince, onion, raisins, pistachios, sugar, honey vinegar, and salt over medium heat. Bring this to a gentle boil and cook until the quince and celeriac are tender, about 10 minutes. Add the cider vinegar, curry, and mustard seeds, remove from the heat, and transfer to the prepared jars.

Cover each with a lid, screw it down tightly, and turn the jars upside down on a wire rack for 5 minutes. After 5 minutes, turn them upright and let them seal. Once sealed, store in a cool, dark pantry for up to 1 year. Keep any jars that don't seal in the refrigerator and use within 1 week.

Refried Mbombo Beans with Plantain

Recently there has been a lot of buzz in the seed world surrounding these beautiful green Mbombo beans from Africa. While the unusual color is undoubtedly a selling point, the green cooks out as soon as the beans are boiled. In fact, they turn slate gray while remaining delightfully tender, even silky smooth, once cooked, whatever their color. Consider this late summer–early fall dish a one-pot meal. Besides boiled plantains, the beans go equally well over rice, pasta, potatoes, or even sweet potatoes.

Serves 6 to 8

12 ounces dried Mbombo beans

4 fresh bay leaves, bruised

4 ounces kale leaves, stems and veins removed

3 large green plantains (about 2 pounds)

1 cup finely chopped onion

1 cup chopped plus 1 tablespoon minced cilantro leaves, separated

¾ cup extra-virgin olive oil

3 tablespoons white wine vinegar

1 tablespoon sea salt

1 tablespoon hot chile powder or *merkén*, or to taste

Grated zest of 1 lime

½ cup chopped sun-dried tomatoes

In a deep work bowl, cover the beans with 2 cups boiling water. Let the beans soak at least 6 hours and up to overnight, until they are fully swollen and most of the water has been absorbed. Transfer the beans and any remaining soaking liquid to a deep stewing pan and cover with 4 cups fresh, unsalted water. Add the bay leaves. Set over medium heat and bring to a simmer. Cook until the beans are tender, about 25 minutes. Drain and set aside, reserving the cooking liquid. Discard the bay leaves.

Bring a large saucepan of water to a boil over medium-high heat. Carefully plunge the kale leaves into the water for 1 minute. Remove with a skimmer or slotted spoon and drain, keeping the water at a boil. Cut each plantain in half crosswise, trim off the ends, and add to the water. Cook until easily pierced with a fork and tender, about 25 minutes.

Gently pat the kale leaves dry. Chop the leaves and transfer them to a food processor or blender, along with the onion, chopped cilantro, ½ cup olive oil, and the vinegar. Puree until smooth. Add 1½ cups of the cooked beans plus 1 cup of the reserved cooking liquid and puree until thick and creamy. Transfer the mixture to a deep work bowl and stir in the remaining beans, salt, chile powder, and lime zest. Drain the plantains. When cool enough to handle, peel the skins and cut the fruit into thick slices on the diagonal. Transfer to a warm serving dish and spoon the refried beans on top. Drizzle with the remaining ¼ cup olive oil and top with the chopped sundried tomatoes and the minced cilantro. Serve immediately.

Saffron Corn Soup

The Pennsylvania Dutch have been cooking with saffron since the 1730s, when it was introduced as a cottage industry. Saffron soon crept into regional cookery and became a classic addition to chicken corn soup. This recipe takes that traditional idea a few steps farther by blending the freshness of sweet corn, fall harvest vegetables, and the rich flavor of saffron into a farmhouse soup with a dash of spicy Merkén sauce. It is the perfect starter soup for Thanksgiving, or the local Pennsylvania Dutch equivalent called Harvest Home; furthermore, it is elegant, light, and easy to make even with vegetable stock.

Serves 6 to 8

4 tablespoons unsalted butter

1 medium onion, coarsely chopped

3 cups thinly sliced leek (white part only)

3 cups grated white sweet corn, cobs reserved

2 cups peeled and chopped potato

6 cups chicken or vegetable stock

½ teaspoon powdered saffron

1 cup finely diced carrot

2 teaspoons sugar, optional (depending on sweetness of corn)

2 teaspoons sea salt, or to taste

1 cup Merkén Sauce (page 73), for serving

Sliced chives, for garnish

In a deep stewing pan, melt the butter over medium heat. Add the onion and leek, cover, and sweat until the vegetables are soft but not changing color, about 5 minutes. Add the grated corn, reserved cobs, potatoes, and stock. Cover and stew until all the ingredients are tender, about 30 minutes. Discard cobs.

Transfer the cooked vegetables and liquid to a food processor or blender and puree until thick and smooth, working in batches if necessary. Transfer to a deep work bowl and stir in the saffron.

Bring a small saucepan of water to a rapid boil over medium-high heat. Add the diced carrot and cook just until tender, about 3 minutes. Drain and add the carrots to the puree. Add the sugar, if using, and salt, and adjust seasoning.

Serve the soup chilled or reheat and serve hot. Dot or drizzle *merkén* sauce over each serving and garnish with chives.

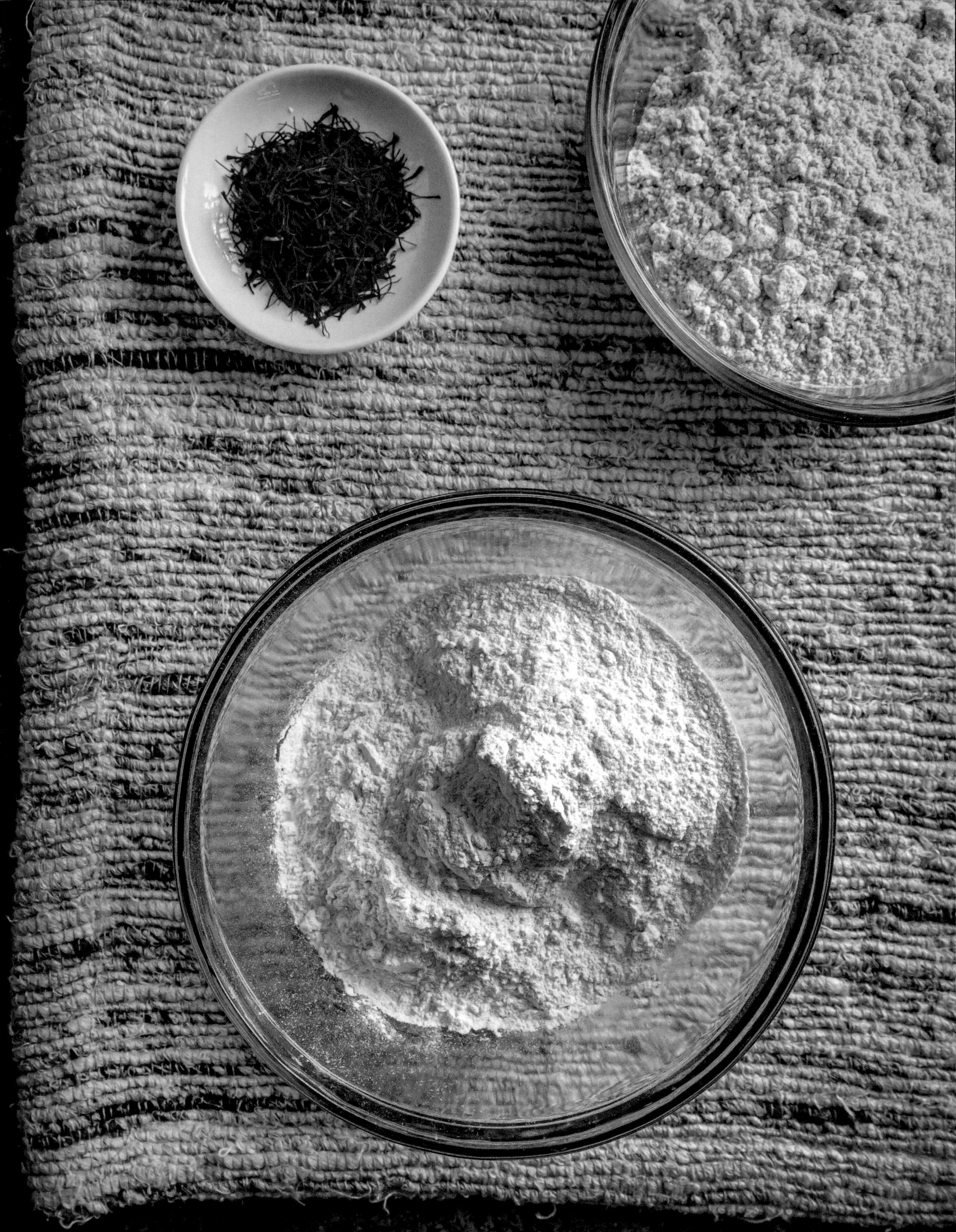

Sorghum Chapatis with Saffron

Due to its height, sorghum may not seem like an appealing plant for the kitchen garden; for certain it could overpower a small plot. All the same, it is gracefully bamboo-like as an ornamental and can be an effective accent in roomy gardens laid out for visual beauty. After experimenting with many varieties of sorghum from different parts of the world, we struck on a landrace from Inner Mongolia, created by local farmers solely as a flour grain (as opposed to processing its stems for syrup). Since sorghum flour lacks gluten and is granular in texture, it is not well adapted to bread baking, but when combined with starchy plantain or cassava flour, makes excellent chapatis. Serve with New Guinea Basil Pesto (page 74), Snake Gourd Curry (page 92), or Kashmiri Collard Chutney (page 122).

Makes 12

1⅓ cups plantain or cassava flour

⅔ cup sorghum flour

1 tablespoon ground coriander

1 teaspoon fine sea salt

½ teaspoon whole cumin seeds

½ teaspoon ground saffron dissolved in 1 cup warm water

2 tablespoons almond, walnut, or sunflower oil

1 cup sesame seeds, for rolling

Ghee or clarified butter, for brushing

In a large work bowl, sift or whisk together the plantain flour, sorghum flour, coriander, salt, and cumin. Make a well in the center of the dry ingredients and add the saffron water and oil. Stir with a large fork, pulling in the dry ingredients from the sides, adding a little more warm water if necessary, until well combined into a soft, pliant dough. Cover with plastic wrap, transfer to the refrigerator, and chill at least 1 hour in the refrigerator. Allow the dough to return to room temperature before rolling out.

Divide the dough into 12 equal portions and roll into balls. Scatter a work surface with the sesame seeds, then flatten and roll out each ball into a 4- to 6-inch round, flipping partway through to cover both sides with sesame seeds.

Heat a heavy griddle or nonstick skillet over medium-high heat until just smoking. Brush the surface lightly with the ghee then add 1 or 2 chapatis, depending on size. Cook until lightly browned, about 30 seconds per side. Repeat with the remaining chapatis. Serve immediately with chutney or a curry.

Wandering Spirits Tamales

Wandering Spirits is a new variety of flour corn created here at Roughwood. It can be used both whole (in the kernel) or as cornmeal and flour. This recipe highlights this flexibility, but you can substitute any flour corn if you wish. Be advised that making tamales requires a good deal of preparation, which is why traditionally they're made in groups or in large amounts for sharing. This is one of those dishes where the whole family can get involved, and once they are made and cooked, the ensuing feast is worth the wait. Rather than steam the tamales, I prefer to bake them in rich broth, which cuts down on some of the work. Once stuffed you can freeze the uncooked tamales, to thaw as needed, or cook the tamales and then freeze, to reheat before serving.

Makes 20 to 25 tamales

1 cup whole Wandering Spirits flour corn kernels

1 cup Wild Pigeon Beans or small pea-sized bean, such as Amish Knuttle

1 cup finely ground Wandering Spirits corn flour or masa harina

½ cup shredded winter squash or pumpkin (use the large holes of a box grater)

1¼ pounds cooked duck breast, diced or shredded, or ground turkey, cooked

1¼ cups chopped baked wild chestnuts (*chinquapins*), recipe follows

1 cup sunflower oil

2 cups chicken or duck stock enhanced with a soup bunch (see page 193)

½ cup sliced scallions

1 tablespoon minced fresh thyme leaves

1 teaspoon freshly ground black pepper

2½ teaspoons sea salt

20 to 25 dried cornhusks (*hojas de maiz para tamal*)

The day before making the tamales, cook the corn and beans. For the corn, bring at least 2 quarts of water to a boil. In a saucepan, cover the corn with boiling water by at least one inch. Let stand 1 hour to soften, then set over medium heat. Bring to a gentle simmer and cook until the corn softens and swells, about 45 minutes, adding more boiling water as needed. Remove from the heat and let stand at room temperature at least 12 hours. For the beans, place them in a separate heatproof work bowl and cover with boiling water. Cover and let stand at room temperature at least 12 hours.

By the next day, the corn should have absorbed most of the water. Add 2 cups fresh water and set over medium heat. Bring to a simmer and cook until the corn is fully tender but not mushy, about 45 minutes. Drain and set aside.

For the beans, drain and rinse them and transfer them to a saucepan with fresh water to cover; do not salt. Set over medium heat, bring to a gentle simmer, and cook until the beans are tender, 25 to 30 minutes. Drain, then transfer to a food processor, reserving 1 cup of whole beans. Puree the beans until thick.

In a deep work bowl combine the cooked corn kernels, reserved whole beans, bean puree, corn flour, squash, cooked duck or turkey, chestnuts, sunflower oil, 1 cup stock, scallions, thyme, black pepper, and salt. Stir until thick. Cover and set aside in the refrigerator to allow the flavors to mature, about 1 hour. While the filling rests, place the cornhusks in a shallow baking dish and pour boiling water over them to rehydrate. Let soak until tender and pliant, about 1 hour.

To fill and assemble the tamales, drain and lightly pat dry the soaked cornhusks. Lay the softened cornhusks flat on a clean work surface. Portion about 2 tablespoons filling in the center of each cornhusk. Roll the leaf cigar-fashion over the filling, fold down the pointed ends of each leaf. Fold the bottom of the leaf upward and tie both ends with kitchen twine. Rolled tamales can be cooked right away, kept in the refrigerator for 3 to 4 days, or frozen for up to 6 months. Bring tamales to room temperature before cooking.

Preheat the oven to 325°F. In an 11 x 17-inch glass or earthenware baking dish, lay 10 to 12 tamales in a single layer along the bottom. Pour 1½ cups of the remaining stock and ½ cup water over the tamales in each pan and cover tightly with foil. Bake until the filling is set and easily pulls away from the cornhusk, about 1½ hours. Serve hot.

To steam the tamales, bring 2 to 3 inches of water to a simmer in a large pot over medium heat. Add a colander or steamer basket to the pot and add the tamales. Cover and steam until filling is set and easily pulls away from the cornhusk, 1½ to 2 hours.

BAKED CHESTNUTS

There can be a certain amount of waste with chestnuts; some may be discolored and should be discarded, and the bitter inner skin is sometimes difficult to remove. None of this becomes obvious until after the chestnuts are baked, so wise cooks might bake at least 2 pounds when needing 1 pound. Any extra can be frozen for later use in stuffings or pastries.

Preheat the oven to 425°F. With a very sharp knife, slice an X in the shell on the rounded end of each chestnut. Spread the nuts on a baking sheet and bake until the skins have pulled back and the chestnuts are soft, 15 to 20 minutes. Since *chinquapins* (wild chestnuts) are small, their baking time is shorter, 12 to 15 minutes. Remove from the oven and, once cool, peel off the shells. You may need a vegetable peeler for some of the most stubborn inner skins. Once the skins have been removed, chop as directed in the recipe.

Winter

Gardening Under the Snow

According to an old Pennsylvania Dutch folktale, when the full moon shines on Christmas Eve, raccoons rise into the clouds and shake out magic dew, which falls on cakes, pies, cookies, and other treats that believers have left outside. Under the magic dew, the treats come alive and dance with the fairies until sunrise—even old white Knuckle Beans set out in pots will turn to gold. If only winter gardening could be that enchanting! And yet there is gold under the snow, as row upon row of Swabian Winter Peas, Lark's Tongue Kale, and Green Glaze Collards stand to vibrant attention in the garden, seemingly no matter how cold the temperature. Wise old farmers in my part of Pennsylvania claim that the white wind of winter purifies the land. It is not a blind, killing wind out of the north if we turn it to our advantage.

For several years I taught workshops at Roughwood devoted to gardening under the snow, and the buffet lunch that accompanied those classes featured all the winter vegetables we harvested that day fresh from the freezing ground; some of the recipes in this section were developed out of those meals. This part of my cookbook is about taking joy from the winter harvest, hot tea, and coming together around the fireplace or the table to talk: humans relating to and caring for each other. Several recipes in this chapter draw their inspiration from Native American foodways and similar traditions of commensality. Parched corn—common in the Pennsylvania Dutch country, but perhaps less easy to find in other regions—featured heavily in the cookery of the Eastern Woodland tribes, and its toasty caramelized flavor is unique.

Aside from celebrating human relationships, this section of the book is also a celebration of Old World winter vegetables, especially turnips and their seemingly endless biodiversity. Turnip cookery yields many pleasant surprises. From skinny purple Hinona Kabu to black French Pardailhans, snowball-like German Teltows, and brilliant red Scarlet Ohnos, there is no shortage of colorful, delicious options. Perhaps the wild card in this group is the rare *Cavolo Navone* from northern Italy, which is genetically a rutabaga; it cooks like a turnip, although the flesh is richer, creamier, and more full-bodied, thus taking well to olive oil and Italian herbs. To create vegetarian dishes that will pass muster on a cold winter day, in some recipes I have dropped out smoked meats in favor of dried, smoked mushrooms (see Note, page 176).

Armenian Stuffed Fermented Cabbage

This deep-winter vegan recipe will reward you with a perfect one-pot dinner that doubles as delicious fare for anyone observing Lent by giving up meat. Traditionally, the dish is also made for Christmas, when it is served with fish. For strict Eastern Church practice, olive oil is used for Christmas while sesame oil replaces it during Lenten fasting. A Cypriot friend discovered this recipe in the old émigré Armenian community in Nicosia. Much of its special flavor comes from the cabbage and the way it is fermented (see page 155). Once I started fermenting cabbage leaves, I soon realized how many versatile uses they had, so now I keep a supply all winter long. You can use them in place of grape leaves for all sorts of wraps, you can boil them with potatoes to make soup, or cook them simply with string beans and ham. This is a celebration dish traditionally assembled by a community or family, so wrangle some extra hands in the kitchen if it appears daunting. I guarantee that no one will complain come time to serve it! Once cooked, stuffed cabbages can be frozen for later use—they will keep for at least a year. Or you can freeze the premade stuffing and make the wraps as needed.

Serves 10 to 12

1¼ cups dried chickpeas

1½ cups brown baking beans, such as Swedish Brown or Tiger's Eye

1¼ cups small brown lentils

1⅓ cups extra-virgin olive oil or sesame oil

2 pounds chopped onions

2 cups #1 (large-grain) bulgur

10 ounces tomato paste

1½ cups finely minced cilantro leaves

1½ cups finely minced parsley leaves

6 tablespoons sweet paprika powder

1 tablespoon ground caraway seeds

Sea salt and freshly ground black pepper

30 fermented cabbage leaves (recipe follows)

Preheat the oven to 250°F. In a large saucepan, bring 12 cups water to a boil over medium-high heat. Cover and adjust temperature to maintain a gentle boil.

In a deep earthenware casserole or baking dish with a lid, cover the dried chickpeas and beans with 6 cups of the boiling water. Cover the pot and bake 2 hours. Remove from the oven and let cool slightly. Carefully drain any cooking liquid left in the pot into a large measuring cup; add water if needed to yield 1½ cups. Set the drained beans and chickpeas aside in a work bowl.

While the beans and chickpeas are baking, cover the lentils with 3 cups boiling water in a saucepan over medium heat and simmer until tender, about 25 minutes. Drain and add the lentils to the beans and chickpeas.

In a broad sauté pan, heat 1 cup of the olive oil over medium heat. Add the chopped onions, stir to coat them with the oil, then cover and sweat until soft, about 8 minutes. Using a slotted spoon, transfer the onions to the beans and chickpeas, leaving the oil in the pan. Add the bulgur, increase heat to medium-high, and stir until it starts to brown lightly and smells toasty, about 5 minutes. Reduce the heat to medium and carefully stir in 3 cups of the boiling water. Cover and cook until all the liquid is absorbed, 10 to 12 minutes, then turn off the heat. Place a clean kitchen towel on top of the pan then re-cover with the lid. Let the bulgur steam until loose and fluffy, 15 to 20 minutes more. Transfer to the bowl with the beans and chickpeas and stir.

In a bowl, dissolve the tomato paste in the 1½ cups reserved chickpea-bean cooking liquid then stir into the beans and chickpeas. Add the cilantro, parsley, paprika, and caraway, season with salt and pepper, and stir. At this point, the filling can be refrigerated overnight. Return to room temperature before stuffing.

Preheat the oven to 325°F. Remove the leaves from the brine, pat dry, and spread flat on a clean work surface. Trim off the base of each leaf. Place a scant ⅓ cup of the stuffing mixture in the center of each leaf. Fold the sides over the stuffing, fold the bottom (stem) end upward, and finally cover this with the top part of the leaf folded downward. Once stuffed, transfer the cabbages seam-side down into an 11 x 17-inch glass baking dish or large earthenware casserole. You can divide them between two smaller baking dishes, but pack them tightly.

Pour 4 cups water (or 3 cups red or white wine plus 1 cup water) over the cabbages, then drizzle with the remaining ⅓ cup olive oil. Lay a sheet of parchment paper on the surface (this helps keep the cabbages submerged during baking) then cover tightly with foil. Bake 1 hour until the stuffed cabbages are firm. Serve hot or at room temperature.

FERMENTED CABBAGE LEAVES

This recipe is by far one of the most flavorful ferments I have tasted and, as a result, I keep these versatile cabbage leaves on hand all winter long. The beauty of the recipe is that it requires only ten days to ferment. You can keep the cabbage in the brine until needed, just store in a cool, dark place once mature. Take note that the ferment should develop a slight milky film on the surface of the brine: a healthy sign that lacto-fermentation is doing its work. Do not be alarmed when you see it; it also tenderizes the cabbage.

Makes 30

¾ cup sea salt

30 large cabbage leaves (from 2 heads of cabbage)

6 garlic cloves

8 fresh bay leaves

1 tablespoon black peppercorns

2 tablespoons whole coriander seeds

10 bushy sprigs dill

In a deep, nonreactive pot, combine the salt and 4 quarts spring water over medium heat and bring to a gentle boil, stirring until the salt is dissolved. Remove from the heat and cool. While the brine cools, rinse the cabbage leaves, pat dry, and transfer them into a 3-gallon stoneware crock or glass preserving jar with a wide mouth. Add the garlic, bay leaves, peppercorns, coriander, and dill.

Pour the brine over then place a porcelain plate on top of the mixture. Set a weight on top of the plate (or use fermentation weights) so that the leaves are fully submerged in the brine. Cover the crock with a lid or with cheesecloth and let sit 10 days at room temperature to ferment, after which time the leaves will have changed color and become tender. Keep in the brine. Like sauerkraut, the cabbage leaves will keep submerged in the brine in the refrigerator up to 1 year.

Crosnes and Radish Marinade

Crosnes (*Stachys affinis*) are rhizome-producing relatives of the medical herb Wood Betony. Their unusual name comes from Crosne, the French village where they were first cultivated in Europe. The plant, which actually originated in China, is a perennial and is also quite popular in Japan under the name *chorogi*. In Japan, crosnes are pickled with red shiso to create a brilliant red condiment for the Lunar New Year. The key coloring ingredient here, watermelon radish, is greenish-white outside but red within, and is available in winter, when red shiso is not in season. You could also use the Scarlet Ohno turnip, which is even redder than the watermelon radish but doesn't have the same flavor. As beautiful as the dish looks, with its vibrant red hue, it's also a complex combination of flavors and textures.

Don't peel the skin on crosnes. It contains much of their sweet, nutty flavor, somewhat akin to chestnuts. You can eat them raw or cooked, but avoid overcooking to spoil their delicate, crunchy texture.

Serves 6 to 8

For the marinade

1½ cups unseasoned rice vinegar

6 tablespoons mirin

¾ cup fish sauce

¾ cup spicy Ginger Vinegar (page 180) or red shiso vinegar

2 teaspoons sea salt

4 2-inch-long strips kombu (dried kelp)

4 wide strips lemon zest, from 1 lemon

For the vegetables

1 pound freshly harvested crosnes, washed and trimmed

8 ounces watermelon radish, trimmed, sliced into thin matchsticks

1 medium carrot (ideally violet or red), pared and thinly sliced

½ cup finely diced red onion

Tosted sesame oil, for serving

In a deep, nonreactive work bowl, combine the marinade ingredients and let sit at room temperature until the kombu softens, about 1 hour.

While the marinade infuses, combine the crosnes, radish, carrot, and onion in a shallow work bowl. Once the kombu is soft, remove it from the marinade and slice into thin strips; remove and discard the zest but reserve the marinade. Add the kombu to the crosnes mixture and pour over the reserved marinade. Cover and refrigerate at least 24 hours and up to 2 days; after 2 days the crosnes begin to lose their crunch and color.

Using a slotted spoon, transfer the vegetables from the marinade to a serving dish. Spoon over some of the marinade then drizzle with sesame oil. Serve at room temperature.

Gaspé Samp Stew

Samp, or cracked corn, was a staple winter food for indigenous peoples throughout the Eastern Woodlands. An unsung culinary treasure, Gaspé corn is miniature enough to be planted in large flowerpots. According to Mi'kmaq oral tradition, it was likely one of the first corns ever seen by Europeans, perhaps even by Vikings, cultivated as far north as Quebec's Gaspé peninsula and modern-day Maine. As an heirloom variety, it remains rare in most kitchen gardens, but it shouldn't be. Roughwood's seed stock comes directly from Mi'kmaq growers in eastern Canada, who also make this unique, traditional porridge. In the supermarket, you'll find another kind of samp sold as white hominy or *morocho partido*. The term morocho means that the cracked corn is a soft, starchy flour corn as opposed to flint, thus it is normally white. True Gaspé corn is a yellow flint variety; as with all flint corns, it requires a longer cooking time than flour varieties. That said, the Native American method for cooking flint corn samp was quite straightforward: the cracked corn was placed in an earthenware pot with water, set down among hot coals, and allowed to simmer continually. Meats and other ingredients were added from time to time, as well as more samp and more water as needed—a true hot pot. People helped themselves when they felt hungry. While this kind of communal one-pot meal sounds ideal for large outdoor gatherings, such as cookouts or picnics, rather than cooking in hot coals you will have excellent results from the oven as directed below. It will have a somewhat fluffy texture, like baked rice.

Serves 8 to 10

3 cups samp or cracked corn (see Note)

2 quarts fish stock or seafood stock

4 ounces salt pork or slab bacon, finely diced

1½ pounds yellow onions, coarsely chopped (about 4 cups)

3 medium potatoes, peeled and cubed

4 ounces cod fillet, cut into bite-size pieces

4 ounces Atlantic salmon fillet, cut into bite-size pieces

8 ounces medium scallops or large scallops, halved to bite-size

3 garlic cloves, minced

½ cup sliced scallions (green and white parts)

½ cup finely chopped parsley leaves

Sea salt

In a colander, rinse the samp until the water runs clear. Transfer to a deep work bowl and cover with 9 cups water. Soak at room temperature at least 12 and up to 24 hours so that it swells—similar to soaking beans.

Drain the samp and transfer to an ovenproof saucepan or small pot. Preheat the oven to 250°F. Cover the corn with 4 cups boiling water. Cover with a tight-fitting lid and bake 2 hours, stirring the corn after 1 hour. Should the water evaporate as the corn swells, add up to 1 additional cup just to keep the corn from scorching. After 2 hours, the corn will have absorbed the liquid and puffed up like rice. If using flint corn, allow 3 hours cooking time.

Transfer the cooked samp into a large stewing pan and add 1 quart stock and stir well to loosen; set aside. In a heavy, deep saucepan or stewing pan over medium heat, render the diced salt pork just until it begins to brown, about 3 minutes. Add the onions, stir well, cover, and sweat until the onions are soft, about 5 minutes. Add the remaining 1 quart fish stock and stir, loosening any browned bits from the bottom of the pan. Remove from heat and transfer the mixture to the cooked samp and stir to combine.

Set the stewing pan with samp over medium heat. Add the potatoes and bring to a gentle boil. Cook just until the potatoes are tender, about 15 minutes. Carefully stir in the cod, salmon, scallops, and garlic and cook just until the fish flakes and the scallops are opaque, about 10 minutes. Add the scallions and parsley and season with salt. Serve immediately.

Mohawk Corn Muffins

This recipe is inspired by and adapted from a traditional Mohawk cornbread recorded in 1910 by anthropologist Arthur Parker. I think most would agree these are by far the most richly flavored corn muffins going, but for the special flavor that takes these winter delicacies into a class by themselves, the secret is traditional corn. First, parched sweet corn is essential. Parched corn are roasted dried corn kernels; they can be used in cooking or snacking. In Pennsylvania, Cope's is the best-known brand (see pageneralstore.com), but chances are you can find locally made versions at a nearby farmers market. The other critical ingredient is the flour corn. Tuscarora, Oneida White, and Mohawk Round Nose are among the best choices (all closely related to Delaware *Puhwem*, since they share a common genetic ancestor).

Makes 10 to 12

½ cup parched (dried) sweet corn (see Note)

1½ cups Tuscarora or Oneida, or Mohawk Round Nose fine white corn flour or masa harina

½ cup all-purpose flour

2 tablespoons baking powder

1½ teaspoons sea salt

¼ cup maple sugar

⅓ cup whole dried blueberries (ideally freeze-dried)

1 large egg

1 cup buttermilk

¼ cup sunflower oil, plus more for the muffin tins

½ cup chopped hickory nuts or pecans

In a deep work bowl, cover the parched sweet corn with 1 cup boiling water. Cover the bowl and let stand about 3 hours or until the corn is completely soft. Drain into a colander or sieve set over a bowl to press out and reserve the liquid. Measure ½ cup, adding water as needed. Set aside.

Preheat the oven to 425°F. In a deep work bowl, sift or whisk together the corn flour, all-purpose flour, baking powder, salt, and maple sugar until thoroughly combined. Fold in the softened parched corn and the dried blueberries. In a separate work bowl, beat the egg until a lemon color and frothy. Add the reserved ½ cup corn soaking liquid, buttermilk, and oil. Make a well in the center of the dry ingredients and stir in the egg mixture to form a thick batter.

Grease muffin tins with sunflower oil and fill the cups about two-thirds full. Scatter chopped nuts on top of each then bake until fully risen, 18 to 20 minutes. Test with a skewer (or broom straw) for doneness. Cool on a rack; serve at room temperature.

Irish Potato Cakes (*Pratie Oaten*)

This simple dish, fit for a nippy winter day, remains one of the easiest and most satisfying ways to run floury heirloom potatoes through their paces. Red Cups, Snowdrop, Flour Ball, Black Champion—these are all old Irish heirloom varieties worth seeking out, while the most well known might be the Irish Lumper, which pre-dates 1770. This is the infamous potato whose widespread failure in the 1840s caused the Great Famine—a stark lesson in the benefits of biodiversity, or the dangers of its lack. Happily, White Peach Blow, an American variety introduced in 1876, is still one of the most productive heirloom varieties. Snowflake, another American classic created in 1874, is remarkable for its large size and fluffy texture when cooked. Seek out local growers for information about which variety to try in your garden.

Many recipes call for butter, but Irish cooks of old also used bacon drippings or just plain lard, whatever they had most handy. Bacon's smokiness imparts great, subtle flavor to the cakes; if cooking on a griddle, you do not need much. The microwave makes shorter work of cooking the potatoes while not leaving them wet, which makes for lighter cakes. Serve these while still hot, with sweet Irish butter or a creamy cheese such as Boursault or Boursin. Incidentally, there are some incredible local cheeses made in Pennsylvania, but they are not widely available.

Makes 16

2 pounds floury potatoes (see Note)

12 tablespoons unsalted butter or bacon drippings, plus more for the griddle

1½ cups cooked steel-cut oatmeal, at room temperature

2 tablespoons potato starch

2 teaspoons sea salt

¼ cup oat flour, plus more for the work surface

Stab each potato 4 to 6 times with a fork and set them on paper towels in a microwave oven. Cook at 80% power for 6 to 7 minutes (depending on your microwave; check your settings for baking potatoes). They should be hot and steaming. Remove potatoes and let cool until comfortable to handle but still warm. Cut potatoes in half lengthwise and scoop out the cooked insides, discarding the jackets.

Mash the potatoes with a fork or run them through a food mill until smooth and fluffy. Mix in the butter and oats while still warm and knead gently until well combined. Sift or whisk together the potato starch, salt, and oat flour and knead into the dough. Dust a clean surface with oat flour then pat or roll the dough out about 1 inch thick. Using a 3-inch round cutter, cut out 16 cakes.

Grease a cast-iron griddle or skillet and set over medium-high heat. Lay the cakes on the hot griddle and brown on both sides until cooked through, 2 to 3 minutes per side. Repeat until all the cakes are browned and crisp. Serve immediately.

Iroquois Bean Bread

The eye-catching Iroquois Bread Bean gives this delicious recipe not just its name, but its unique texture and flavor. For best results, use two heavy loaf pans measuring about 4½ by 9½ inches and at least 2 inches deep. You can also bake this bread Pennsylvania farmhouse-style in 9-inch round cake pans or pie plates—this recipe makes 3. Its texture resembles zucchini bread or carrot cake and can even be toasted. It makes an admirable coffee cake and is excellent when served hot with maple syrup. You can also freeze it for several months to have on hand for company.

Makes 2 loaves or 3 round cakes

10 ounces dried Iroquois Bread Beans (about 1½ cups)

2 cups parched sweet corn

1½ cups coarsely chopped scallions (white and green parts)

1 cup Tuscarora or Oneida white corn flour or fine white masa harina

2 cups all-purpose flour

½ cup maple sugar or organic sugar

2 tablespoons baking powder

2 tablespoons sea salt

4 large eggs, whites and yolks separated

¼ cup sunflower oil, plus more for baking pans

2 cups sour cream or buttermilk

Yellow cornmeal or polenta, for baking pans

In a heatproof work bowl, cover the dried beans with 2 cups boiling water and soak until most of the liquid is absorbed, at least 4 hours. While the beans are soaking, in a second bowl, cover the dried sweet corn with 2 cups boiling water and let soak until most of the liquid is absorbed, about 2 hours.

Transfer the swollen beans with any remaining liquid to a deep stewing pan. Add 3 cups water and set over medium heat. Bring to a simmer and cook until the beans are soft and easily mashed with a fork, about 35 minutes. Transfer to a food processor and puree into a coarse paste. Transfer to a deep work bowl and stir in the soaked sweet corn and chopped scallions.

Preheat the oven to 375°F. Sift or whisk together the corn flour, all-purpose flour, maple sugar, baking powder, and salt, making certain the baking powder is evenly distributed. Fold the dry ingredients into the bean mixture to form a stiff, crumbly paste.

In a separate bowl, beat the egg yolks until light and frothy. Stir in the sunflower oil and sour cream until thoroughly combined. Fold the yolk mixture into the paste to form a batter. In another work bowl, beat the egg whites until stiff peaks form, then gently fold them into the batter. Grease the pans with oil and dust generously with cornmeal. Pour the batter into the pans and bake in the preheated oven until fully risen in the center and turning golden on top, 40 to 45 minutes. For round cake pans or pie plates, bake at the same oven temperature for approximately 30 minutes. Remove from the oven and cool on racks.

Nantucket Corn Cake

I have tried this recipe with many types of cornmeal, but the best result always turns out to be made with flour corn—Iroquois Purple, Gourd Seed Corn, Tuscarora or Oneida Flour Corns, and especially Delaware Puhwem Corn all yield superior results. Historical recipes usually require adjustment since modern cornmeal tends to be denser than earlier hand-ground versions. The secret then is in the double sifting. In truth, even if you follow the recipe and use masa harina, this recipe will not disappoint, producing a soft, cake-like texture unlike the coarse and grainy bite more often associated with Southern cornbread.

This excellent heirloom recipe came from Maria Mitchell (1818–1889), a Quaker born on Nantucket, as recorded in a circa-1840s manuscript cookbook once belonging to the Walton family of Newtown, Pennsylvania. While Mitchell found renown as an astronomer, much less has been written about her culinary output. This corn cake is best when eaten hot from the oven with fresh butter and Nantucket beach plum jam.

Serves 8 to 10

Vegetable oil, for the pan

2 cups sifted Tuscarora or Oneida, or Mohawk Round Nose fine white cornmeal or masa harina

⅔ cup sifted whole wheat flour

⅓ cup sifted all-purpose flour

1 teaspoon sea salt

1 tablespoon baking powder

3 tablespoons superfine sugar

2 large eggs, whites and yolks separated

2 cups buttermilk

Preheat the oven to 425°F. Grease a 10-inch cast-iron skillet or earthenware baking dish with a 2-inch rim. Set aside.

Sift the cornmeal into a deep work bowl (this should be its second sifting; see Note) then remove and set aside 2½ tablespoons. In a separate bowl, sift the whole wheat flour and discard the bran. Add the sifted flour to the cornmeal then repeat with the all-purpose flour. Add the salt, baking powder, and sugar and sift or whisk the cornmeal mixture again.

In a separate work bowl, beat the egg yolks until light and frothy and add the buttermilk. Make a well in the center of the dry ingredients and gently stir in the egg mixture until the batter is smooth. In another bowl, whisk the egg whites until stiff peaks form. Carefully fold the egg whites into the batter until just combined. Pour the batter into the prepared skillet and bake until fully risen in the center and turning golden on top, 30 to 35 minutes. Cool slightly on a rack and serve warm.

Parched Corn Waffles with Ham and Bean Gravy

This delicious recipe represents a new take on an old Pennsylvania Dutch winter classic. We use a lot of dried corn from the garden during cold weather and the toasty flavor of parched sweet corn is unique. I first tested this recipe in an old-time Griswold Number 9 "American" waffle iron, patented in 1908. While I don't expect you to cook with an antique, the point is that you really want your waffles to turn out crispy—closely follow the instructions for your particular waffle iron. Soggy waffles and hot gravy are not a match made in culinary heaven; if your waffles are not crisp, warm them in a low oven for a few minutes, and once hot never stack them: their own steam will turn them soft. Don't forget that you can also freeze the waffles and the cooked gravy and use them as needed at a later time.

Serves 4 to 6

Ham and Bean Gravy (recipe follows)

1 cup parched sweet corn (see Note, page 161)

4 large eggs, whites and yolks separated

1½ cups buttermilk

¼ cup vegetable oil

1¾ cups pastry flour

1 tablespoon baking powder

½ teaspoon baking soda

½ teaspoon sea salt

¾ cup chopped hickory nuts (optional)

In a spice mill or grinder, process the parched sweet corn to fine powder, in batches if necessary. In a medium bowl, beat the egg yolks until light and frothy. Stir in the buttermilk and oil. In another large bowl, sift or whisk together the powdered corn, pastry flour, baking powder, baking soda, and salt until well combined (if sifting, sift 3 times). Add the egg yolk mixture and stir to form a thick batter. In a separate bowl, whisk the egg whites until stiff peaks form. Gently fold the egg whites into the batter. Set the batter aside to rest, about 5 minutes.

While the batter rests, heat a waffle iron until hot. Add the batter, ½ cup at a time, until most of the surface is covered. Spread the batter ½ inch from the edge, close the lid and bake until golden and crispy. Repeat until all the batter is used.

Serve immediately with ham and bean gravy. Sprinkle chopped hickory nuts over each serving, if using.

HAM AND BEAN GRAVY

For the best flavor, be certain that your bay leaves are fresh to suffuse the gravy with their fragrance. You can add other herbs, such as minced parsley or lovage. A dash of cayenne pepper in place of the white pepper adds an intriguing heat.

Serves 4 to 6

1 cup dried Railroad Beans or heirloom pinto beans

3 tablespoons unsalted butter

8 ounces ham steak, diced (about the size of corn kernels)

⅓ cup sliced scallions (white and green parts)

3 tablespoons finely diced green bell pepper

3 tablespoons finely diced celery

1 cup organic fire-roasted sweet corn (see Note, page 131)

6 fresh bay leaves

2 cups heavy cream or plain yogurt

2 teaspoons potato starch

½ teaspoon freshly grated nutmeg, or to taste

2 teaspoons minced thyme or savory leaves (optional)

Sea salt and freshly ground white pepper

In a deep work bowl, cover the beans with 2 cups boiling water. Soak until fully swollen, at least 6 hours. Drain and rinse the beans, then transfer to a stewing pan. Add 3 cups water (do not add salt or it will toughen the beans). Set over medium heat, bring to a gentle boil, and cook until the beans are soft, 25 to 30 minutes. Drain and set aside.

In a medium-sized sauté pan, heat the butter over medium heat. Add the ham and stir until lightly browned and crisp, about 5 minutes. Add the scallions, green pepper, celery, fire-roasted corn, and bay leaves. Cover and sweat until the vegetables soften, about 4 minutes. Add the reserved beans and cover until heated through.

In a separate saucepan, heat the cream over medium heat. Whisk in the potato starch and bring the cream just to a gentle boil to thicken. Stir in the nutmeg, then pour over the ham and bean mixture. Stir in the thyme, adjust seasoning, and serve hot over the waffles.

Pennsylvania Succotash

This recipe celebrates three classic Pennsylvania heirloom beans, Dr. Martin's Lima (developed in the 1920s by dentist Dr. Harold Martin), the Indian Hannah Pole Bean, (a Native American variety associated with a Lenape, Hannah Freeman), and the meaty brown Spelt Bean (*Dinkelbuhn*), a Pennsylvania Dutch variety from Lancaster County. The dish's basic idea is to combine three types of beans, each with a distinctive texture and appearance: the jumbo lima features an unusual sweetness; Indian Hannah has a pleasing smoky flavor; and the Spelt Bean could pass for grain, hence the name. Soaking and cooking the three types of beans separately may appear inconvenient but will ensure evenly tender beans. Because they are different types, if soaked or cooked together one will always end up too firm or too soft. For fresh or frozen beans, blanch in boiling water just until crisp-tender and hot.

Serves 4 to 6

1 cup dried Dr. Martin's Lima (or lima of your choice)

1 cup dried Indian Hannah Pole Bean (or speckled pinto-type bean of your choice)

¾ cup dried Spelt Bean (or small brown bean of your choice)

1 cup cooked wild rice

3 cups frozen organic fire-roasted sweet corn, thawed (see Note, page 131)

½ cup chopped scallions (white and green parts)

¼ cup diced red bell pepper

½ teaspoon dried savory or thyme

1 cup toasted walnut oil

¼ cup shallot vinegar or white wine vinegar

Sea salt and freshly ground black pepper

In a large pot, bring 12 cups water to a boil over medium-high heat.

In a deep work bowl, cover the dried lima beans with 4 cups boiling water. Repeat with the pole and spelt beans in separate bowls. Let the beans soak until fully swollen, at least 2 to 2½ hours (the limas will take the longest). Strain and transfer the beans to three separate saucepans. Add 4 cups fresh water to each saucepan, set over medium heat, and bring to a gentle simmer. Cook until tender, 20 to 25 minutes. Once tender, drain and combine the beans in a large bowl. Add the cooked wild rice, corn, scallions, red pepper, and savory, and stir until well mixed.

In a small bowl, whisk together the oil and vinegar until combined and season with salt and pepper. Pour the dressing over the bean mixture while still warm. Stir well to mix then season with salt and pepper. Serve warm or at room temperature.

Picard Turnip Soup

Picardy remains one of my favorite corners of northern France. This cold, windy region close to Belgium is the perfect place to explore recipes for the winter table: The Péronne Turnip (*Navet de Péronne*) is a delicate French heirloom variety featuring a fat taproot and rosy-hued shoulders. We want to emphasize the sweetness of freshly harvested turnips, which white carrots, leeks, and wine all do. Historic recipes call for *saguette*, a medieval white wine from Picardy made with honey and sage; today, a white *vinho verde* such as Alvarinho will give the right balance of acid and sweetness.

Never throw away turnip skins. These practical parings can be dried in a food dehydrator, like fruit or fresh herbs, and pulverized into a powder. This seasoning makes an excellent base for stocks and soups, especially handy in vegetarian cooking.

Serves 6 to 8

2½ pounds Péronne Turnips (*Navet de Péronne*) or white turnips, peeled and diced (see Note)

½ pound white carrots, peeled and diced

½ pound leeks, white parts only, washed and thinly sliced

3 tablespoons duck fat or unsalted butter, at room temperature

2 cups *vinho verde* or medium-dry white wine

6 cups vegetable stock enhanced with a soup bunch (see page 193)

2 cups dry hard cider, or to taste

Minced chervil, for garnish

Preheat the oven to 375°F. In a deep earthenware casserole, combine the diced turnips, white carrots, leeks, and duck fat. Stir to coat. Add the wine and 2 cups vegetable stock. Cover with the lid or tightly with foil and bake until the vegetables are soft, about 1 hour. Remove from the oven, uncover, and let cool.

Transfer the cooled vegetables plus any liquid to a blender or food processor. Add the remaining 4 cups vegetable stock and puree until smooth and creamy. Pour into a clean saucepan and add the cider, plus more if you prefer a thinner soup. Reheat carefully over medium heat just until hot. Serve immediately with minced chervil.

Roughwood Green Glaze Collards with Peanut Dressing

The original Green Glaze Collards were introduced in 1820 by Philadelphia seedsman David Landreth. This variety is completely resistant to cabbage worms (due to the glaze on the leaves), overwinters well, and, best of all, is as tender as spinach. We have been growing it at Roughwood for many years and it provides us with greens from October to April. As an experiment, I crossed it with a medieval cabbage from Flanders, resulting in a new strain of our own featuring purple stems, which produces little heads about the size of carnations up and down the stems each spring. They are a wonderful addition to the winter table. Use whatever variety of collard greens is available locally—the younger and fresher the greens, the better.

Serves 8 to 10

For the peanut dressing:

½ cup creamy peanut butter

1 cup Ginger Vinegar (page 180) or white balsamic vinegar

¼ cup fish sauce

2 tablespoons finely minced cilantro leaves

Grated zest of 2 limes

For the collard greens:

3 tablespoons peanut oil

2 tablespoons minced garlic

1 pound collard greens (see Note), stems removed, chopped into bite-size pieces

¼ cup fish sauce

Chopped toasted unsalted peanuts, for garnish

Prepare the dressing by combining the peanut butter and ginger vinegar in a small work bowl. Whisk vigorously to emulsify the ingredients, then add the fish sauce, cilantro, and grated lime zest.

In a wok or well-seasoned cast-iron skillet, heat the oil over medium-high heat. When the oil begins to smoke and crackle, add 1 tablespoon minced garlic and stir until the garlic starts to turn golden, 1 to 2 minutes, then add the chopped greens. Stir and cover, letting the greens cook about 2 minutes. Add ½ cup water, stir well to redistribute the greens, and replace the cover. Reduce heat to medium and sweat, stirring once or twice, about 5 minutes. Add the fish sauce, stirring to coat thoroughly. Once the collards have turned bright green and are tender, after about 10 minutes, stir in the remaining 1 tablespoon garlic.

Serve immediately. Drizzle individual servings with peanut dressing and garnish with chopped peanuts.

Pickled Turnips with Quail Eggs

Just as tomatoes are poems of summer, so are turnips sonnets of winter. Each variety has its own unique character. For this recipe, I prefer the delicate German Teltower or *Schneeball* (Snowball) varieties because they are easy to grow, mature quickly, and can be stored in a cold room for several months. Seaweed provides a visual accent that also enhances the sweetness of the pickle's turnips and carrots with its naturally occurring glutamate (the key ingredient in MSG). The unique flavor of rock samphire is more memorable than parsley, being slightly more alkaline with a hint of sour orange. The ingredients all work together to produce a truly elegant condiment that will enhance any game dinner of quail, pheasant, or duck.

Makes 2 quarts

40 strands dried sea palm (*Postelsia palmaeformis*) or similar seaweed

2 pounds small white turnips, peeled and diced

2 to 3 large carrots, peeled, sliced, and cut into ornamental shapes

20 quail eggs, hard-cooked and peeled

4 wide strips lemon or orange zest

1 medium onion, cut in half lengthwise, then sliced paper-thin

1 bunch fresh rock samphire (discard hard stems)

4 fresh bay leaves

3¼ cups white wine vinegar

1 cup organic sugar

2 tablespoons pickling salt or sea salt

In a small work bowl cover the seaweed with 2 cups boiling water. Let stand until fully reconstituted and tender, about 4 hours.

While the seaweed softens, in a large pot bring 6 cups water to a gentle boil over medium-high heat. Add the diced turnips and cook just until tender and heated through, 4 to 5 minutes. With a slotted spoon, transfer the turnips to a strainer or colander and rinse with cold water, keeping the pot at a gentle boil. Set aside the turnips aside. Repeat with the carrot slices, poaching 3 to 4 minutes. Strain and set aside.

When the seaweed is tender, drain and combine with the poached turnips, carrots, hard-cooked quail eggs, orange zest, sliced onions, and rock samphire in a deep mixing bowl and mix thoroughly.

Bring a large pot of water to a boil and sterilize 1 2-quart canning jar, lid, and ring (or smaller jars with lids and rings). Remove and stand the jar in a shallow roasting pan lined with a clean dishtowel (to prevent sliding). Add enough hot water to come just 1 or 2 inches up the sides of the jar. Place 2 bay leaves at the bottom of the jar then add the turnip mixture. Top with the remaining bay leaves (if using smaller jars, divide the bay leaves and turnip mixture evenly).

Combine 1½ cups spring water, vinegar, sugar, and salt in a deep, nonreactive preserving pan over medium-high heat. Bring to a rolling boil for 3 minutes then pour the brine over the vegetables. Close the jar with the prepared lid, and screw down tightly with the ring. Turn the jar upside down 5 minutes, then turn upright and let cool. The lid should pop downward, indicating the seal, within a few minutes. Store in the refrigerator for up to 2 months.

Roughwood Green Glaze Collards with Smoked Mushrooms and Choclo

In an attempt to try something new with collards, I began experimenting with smoked mushrooms to see how they would fare in place of meat. Our mushroom grower walked me through the complex issues around smoking mushrooms, one of the most significant being that as mushrooms smoke, they also dry out and thus lose their ability to absorb flavors. Ultimately, we found that King Trumpet Mushrooms smoke the best, coming close to bacon in flavor; you can order them directly from Food Hedge Farm (see page 201).

Choclo, one of the other key ingredients in this dish, is a type of corn with gigantic kernels developed more than one thousand years ago by the indigenous peoples of the high Andes. While Roughwood has several sorts in its corn collection, being an equatorial high-altitude variety it is not easy to grow in North America. It can often be found frozen, however, in Latin or South American markets. Substitute hominy if you cannot find choclo.

Serves 4 to 6

2 ounces smoked dried mushrooms (see page 201)

¼ cup extra-virgin olive oil

2 tablespoons unsalted butter

1½ cups coarsely chopped onions

1 tablespoon brown sugar

2 cups white choclo (see Note) or hominy

4 fresh bay leaves

8 ounces collard greens (see Note, page 173), stems trimmed, coarsely chopped

1 teaspoon minced fresh thyme leaves

1½ teaspoons sea salt, or to taste

2 tablespoons tarragon-flavored vinegar (optional)

In a saucepan, bring 4 cups water to a boil over medium-high heat. Pour the water over the mushrooms in a deep work bowl. Cover the bowl and let the mushrooms steep until completely soft, up to overnight. The next day, strain out the mushrooms, reserving 2 cups soaking liquid. Chop the mushrooms into bite-size pieces and set aside.

In a deep stewing pan, heat the oil and butter over medium-low heat. Add the onions and brown sugar and stir well, cover, and sweat just until soft, about 5 minutes. Add the choclo and bay leaves and continue sweating the vegetables, covered, until the choclo softens, about 4 minutes. Add the chopped mushrooms, reserved mushroom soaking liquid, cover, and cook until the mushrooms are heated through, another 10 minutes. Add the chopped collard greens and thyme. Cover and cook until the greens are tender, about 6 to 8 minutes. Adjust seasoning and sprinkle with tarragon vinegar, if using. Serve hot or at room temperature.

Spicy Turnips in Ginger Marinade

For this recipe, the specific variety is less important than choosing turnips of uniform size—smaller ones are better for this recipe, both for their sweetness and eye appeal. I prefer heirloom varieties, such as German Snowball or English White Egg, but fine Japanese varieties like white Tokinashi will also work perfectly. You can even use the marinade with radishes if you are not a fan of turnips. Choose heirloom red onions, such as Red Wethersfield or Cipolla di Tropea, which are always much sweeter than the monsters sold in supermarkets. For best results, use a vegetable slicer or mandoline to shave the turnips and onions paper-thin.

There will be leftover marinade that can be recycled as dressing for summer vegetables, such as zucchini, summer squash, poached carrots, beets, or even basic greens. Store in the refrigerator up to 3 months for use in vinaigrettes and pickle brines or as a marinade for meat, fish, or raw vegetables.

Serves 8 to 10

1¾ pounds small to medium turnips (see Note), trimmed and peeled

6 cups Ginger Vinegar (recipe follows)

2 garlic cloves, minced

2 tablespoons finely grated fresh ginger

¼ cup plus 2 tablespoons fish sauce

¼ cup organic sugar

1 tablespoon sliced hot peppers, such as Thai or serrano

1 pound small red onions (ideally the same size as the turnips)

6 tablespoons toasted sesame oil

2 tablespoons black and white sesame seeds

Sliced Thai or serrano peppers, as garnish (optional)

Using a mandoline or very sharp knife, shave the turnips crosswise as thinly as possible. Bring a pot of water to a gentle boil over medium heat. Using a colander or steamer basket (to make the slices easy to remove), add the turnip slices to the boiling water and cook until just crisp-tender and heated through, 5 to 6 minutes. The precise cooking time will depend on the variety of turnip, so test one for doneness. Remove the colander or steamer basket from the pot and thoroughly drain the poached turnips. Transfer to a shallow bowl. In a medium bowl, combine 3 cups ginger vinegar, garlic, ginger, ¼ cup fish sauce, and sugar, stirring until the sugar is fully dissolved. Pour the marinade over the turnips and stir in the hot peppers. Cover the bowl and let stand 3 days in the refrigerator.

Slice the onions, approximately the same thickness as the turnips, and transfer to a medium bowl or clean jar. Cover with the remaining 3 cups ginger vinegar (onions must be completely submerged in the vinegar). Cover and let stand 3 days in a cool, dark place.

After 3 days, drain the turnips (reserve the marinade, see Note), and repeat with the onions. Chop the marinated turnips and onions into quarters, separating the onions into partial rings, and combine in a bowl or serving dish. In a small bowl, whisk 1 cup of the reserved onion marinade with the sesame oil and 2 tablespoons fish sauce until emulsified. Drizzle the dressing over the turnips and onions. Scatter with the sesame seeds and garnish with hot peppers, if using. Serve at room temperature.

GINGER VINEGAR

As a matter of habit, I make several staggered batches of this vinegar to have on hand when I need it, rather than waiting for each to mature. This vinegar is highly adaptable and can be incorporated into salad dressings, marinades, or anywhere a little spicy acidity would wake up the flavors in a dish.

Makes 6 cups

8 ounces fresh ginger

4 to 6 hot peppers, to taste

4 fresh bay leaves

6 cups white wine vinegar

Sliced ginger, for the bottle (optional)

Bring a large stockpot of water to a boil. Sterilize a 2-quart canning jar and lid in the boiling water. Set aside.

Peel the ginger and slice thinly lengthwise. Transfer to the prepared jar. Cut the peppers in half lengthwise, leaving the seeds for additional heat to taste. Add the halved peppers and bay leaves to the jar. Cover with the vinegar and seal tightly with the lid. Set the jar aside in a cool, dark spot for 30 days to infuse the vinegar. When ready, strain the vinegar into a clean pitcher or saucepan, discard the vegetables, and pour the strained vinegar into sterilized bottles. If desired, add thinly sliced fresh ginger to the bottle to add a nice hit of fresh ginger flavor; however, it will lose potency and look a little shriveled after 2 months. Capped tightly, the vinegar will keep at room temperature at least 1 year.

Sunchoke *Schales*

Pronounced "shah-less," a *schales* is an old Pennsylvania Dutch term for a flat vegetable pie without crust. The word means "shell" and takes its name from the dish in which it is baked. Traditional potters in Pennsylvania still make them; they are about twelve inches in diameter and an inch or two deep. This recipe recalls farmhouse-cookery days when dishes on the common table were shared together as a one-pot meal. Schales has recently undergone something of a revival because it is easy to prepare and can be made from whatever you have on hand. Enjoy as a light winter meal with a crisp white wine, and dream of the coming spring.

Serves 6 to 8

4 ounces stemmed and coarsely chopped dandelion greens, mustard greens, or winter collard greens

4 ounces coarsely chopped Swiss chard (stems and leaves)

2 medium onions, cut in half lengthwise and sliced paper-thin

1 large carrot, pared and shredded

8 ounces sunchokes, trimmed (do not peel) and shredded

2 tablespoons minced fresh sage

2 tablespoons minced fresh thyme leaves

3 garlic cloves, minced

¾ cup grated Parmesan cheese

4 large eggs

1 teaspoon ground ginger

½ cup breadcrumbs

Vegetable oil, for the baking dish

Sea salt and freshly ground black pepper

Preheat the oven to 375°F. In a deep work bowl, combine the chopped dandelion greens, chopped chard, onions, carrot, sunchokes, sage, thyme, garlic, and ½ cup of the Parmesan. In a small bowl, beat the eggs until a lemon color and frothy. Mix in the ginger then fold the eggs into the vegetable mixture along with 2 cups water.

Brush a 2-quart casserole dish or 12-inch tart pan with oil and dust with ¼ cup breadcrumbs. Spread the vegetable mixture evenly in the baking dish and pat smooth. Combine the remaining ¼ cup grated cheese and ¼ cup breadcrumbs and scatter over the top. Bake, uncovered, until golden brown on top and set in the middle, about 45 minutes. Serve immediately.

Swabian Winter Pea Soup

This soup has a nutty, almost chocolate-like flavor and makes excellent gravy poured over boiled potatoes liberally garnished with chopped chives. The unusual flavor is buried in the winter peas, which are reddish brown, quite the opposite of your typical split pea soup. Furthermore, the plants themselves overwinter, so not only do they supply the table with pea shoots, you may even find a few green pods on the vines right there under the snow. Regarding the cooking time of the peas, because this variety is medieval and rock hard when dry, they need long stewing at a low temperature to tenderize properly. If you have a pressure cooker, you can cut the cooking time, but follow the manufacturer's directions for dried beans. Because of their unique flavor, I find that walnut dumplings really take this soup over the top (recipe follows), especially when fried.

Serves 8 to 10

Walnut dumplings (recipe follows)

2 tablespoons unsalted butter

2 tablespoons whole-wheat flour

1 cup chopped celery (with leaves)

½ cup thinly sliced leek (white parts only)

Grated zest of 1 lemon

3 whole cloves

4 fresh bay leaves

4 cups dark stout (brown beer)

4 cups mushroom or vegetable stock, plus more as needed

2 cups dried winter peas

3 garlic cloves, chopped

2 tablespoons minced fresh sage

¼ cup toasted walnut oil

Sour cream and chopped fresh mint, for garnish

In a deep stewing pan, heat the butter and flour over medium heat, stirring, until the mixture begins to foam. Add the celery, leek, lemon zest, cloves, and bay leaves, stirring to coat. Add the stout and mushroom stock, then increase heat to medium-high. Bring to a full boil and cook 5 minutes, then remove from the heat. Let cool, then transfer, covered, to the refrigerator overnight to let the flavors mature.

Next day, return the vegetables and stock to room temperature then strain, discarding the vegetables. Add more mushroom stock or water as needed to measure 8 cups total. Preheat the oven to 250°F. In a heavy earthenware baking dish, combine the peas and 4 cups stock. Cover with a tight-fitting lid or foil and bake until the peas are as soft as cooked potatoes, about 2 hours and 40 minutes. Transfer the cooked peas and their cooking liquid to a food processor or blender. Add the garlic, sage, and remaining 4 cups stock and puree until thick. Press the mixture through a conical strainer or chinoise into a saucepan to further smooth the mixture until the texture resembles thick cream, discarding solids. Add the walnut oil.

Set over medium-low heat until hot. Add the walnut dumplings and stir just until heated through. Serve hot in warmed bowls. Drizzle sour cream over each serving and garnish with mint.

WALNUT DUMPLINGS

These are best made the day before, since overnight storage tenderizes the dumpling crust without hurting the flavor or texture of the dumplings. If starting with whole walnuts, grind until the walnut meal resembles coarse flour. A coffee or spice grinder will often achieve a finer and more even texture than a food processor. Purchased walnut meal can be ground more finely to achieve the flour-like texture.

Makes 48

2½ cups finely ground walnut meal (see Note)

½ cup dried breadcrumbs or panko

½ teaspoon sugar

½ teaspoon ground mace or freshly grated nutmeg

1 tablespoon baking powder

2 large eggs

⅔ cup buttermilk

2 cups saltine cracker crumbs (from 24 crackers crushed with a rolling pin)

2 quarts vegetable oil, for frying (optional)

In a deep work bowl, combine the walnut meal, breadcrumbs, sugar, mace, and baking powder. In a separate bowl, beat the eggs until a lemon color and frothy, then add the buttermilk and mix until smooth. Stir the egg mixture into the dry ingredients to form a crumbly dough.

Using your hands, break off pieces of the dough and roll them into small rounds about the same size as walnuts in the shell. Roll in the cracker crumbs to coat and stand, uncovered, 25 minutes to let dry.

Heat the oil in a deep fryer or large Dutch oven to 375°F. Carefully add the dumplings in batches and fry until golden brown, about 2 minutes. Drain on a paper towel–lined plate and set aside to cool. Best when stored overnight in the refrigerator.

Trentino Rutabaga Polenta *alla Casalenga*

This farmhouse recipe uses *cavolo navone*, a type of rutabaga from the region around Trento in Northeastern Italy. It is thought to date to Roman times, and unlike many rutabagas, the root part grows mostly above ground and resembles an elongated pear. Some varieties have white skins, others dark purple, but the flesh is generally butter-yellow and its flavor reminiscent of sweet potato. The vegetable is biennial—meaning it is better the second year before it blooms and runs to seed, a challenge for gardeners who do not have root cellars. So, if you're not set up to grow this culinary rarity, substitute fresh rutabagas from your local farmers market.

Key to the dish's final texture is to cook the polenta until it achieves the consistency of mashed potatoes; otherwise, when combined with the vegetable puree, it will turn out soft and impossible to slice. These are also delicious topped with Roughwood Tomato Sauce (page 89), Merkén Sauce (page 73), or fresh herbs and Parmesan cheese.

Serves 10 to 20

1 large rutabaga (about 2 pounds), peeled and cubed

6 cups thinly sliced leeks (white part only, from 3 to 4 large)

2 quarts vegetable stock enhanced with a soup bunch (see page 193)

4 fresh bay leaves

3 cups polenta or yellow corn grits

1 cup grated Parmesan cheese

2 tablespoons dried oregano

2 teaspoons minced fresh rosemary

2 tablespoons sea salt

½ cup extra-virgin olive oil, plus more for brushing

2 cups dried breadcrumbs, cornmeal, or a mixture of both

Vegetable oil, for frying

In a deep stewing pan, combine the rutabaga, leeks, stock, and bay leaves over medium heat. Bring to a simmer and cook until the rutabaga is soft, 40 to 50 minutes. Discard the bay leaves, then transfer the cooked vegetables and stock to a blender or food processor. Puree until thick and smooth, in batches if necessary; set aside.

In a small bowl, combine 1 cup polenta with 1 cup hot water and stir until creamy (this step prevents the polenta from becoming lumpy). In a deep stewing pan, heat 5 cups water over medium. Stir in the moistened polenta and the remaining 2 cups polenta. Cook the polenta, stirring, until very thick, about 30 minutes. Stir in the reserved vegetable puree, Parmesan cheese, oregano, rosemary, salt, and olive oil. Bring the mixture just to a slow simmer and cook until thick, 25 to 30 minutes.

Brush a loaf pan or small baking dish with olive oil. Transfer the polenta mixture into the prepared pan and let cool on a rack. Turn the polenta out onto a work surface and slice thickly. Dust slices with breadcrumbs to coat.

Coat a cast-iron skillet or griddle with oil and heat over medium. Brown the polenta slices on both sides till crispy and golden, 2 to 3 minutes per side. Serve hot.

Tarbes Cassoulet with Smoked Mushrooms

The hidden byways of rural French cooking are often full of surprises, and the special cassoulet of Tarbes made with duck and baby limas is unique both in flavor and texture. Happily, you can grow the rare Tarbes lima bean (see page 201) or substitute easy-to-find white baby limas instead. I think one of the secrets of this cassoulet is the duck fat, which rises to the top and melts into the breadcrumbs to form a crust many consider the very best part of the whole dish. The other secret is in the beans, the *haricot Tarbais* from Gascony. Smoked mushrooms replace traditional duck confit for flavor and texture. Using cooked duck or even rotisserie chicken can save time. As with all cassoulet recipes, the effort put in shows in the finished dish. Serve with a luscious red French wine.

Serves 6 to 8

3 ounces smoked King Trumpet mushrooms (see Note, page 176)

2 pounds dried *haricots Tarbais* or small dried lima beans

Sea salt

4 tablespoons duck fat

1½ pounds country-style pork ribs (about 6), cut crosswise into 2-inch pieces with a cleaver (or ask your butcher)

2½ cups coarsely chopped cooked duck

2 cups finely chopped onions

4 cups duck stock or chicken stock

4 garlic cloves, minced

2 tablespoons minced thyme leaves

1 cup dried breadcrumbs

Sea salt and freshly ground black pepper

Sliced scallions or chopped garlic chives, for garnish

In a deep work bowl, cover the smoked mushrooms with 4½ cups boiling water. Cover and let stand overnight. The next day, strain out the mushrooms, reserving 4 cups liquid. Chop the mushrooms into bite-size pieces and set aside.

In a deep work bowl, cover the beans with 8 cups boiling water. Cover and let stand until fully swollen, about 1 hour. Drain and transfer to a saucepan. Add fresh water to cover by 1 inch then season with salt. Set over medium heat, bring to a gentle simmer, and cook until the beans are just tender but not soft, 45 to 50 minutes. Drain and set aside. While the beans are cooking, preheat the oven to 325°F.

In a large Dutch oven or enameled cast-iron casserole, heat the duck fat over medium heat. Add the ribs and brown on all sides, 5 to 6 minutes. Once the meat has begun to brown, add the duck and continue browning the meats for 5 minutes, stirring from time to time. Add the chopped onions, cover, and sweat, taking care not to scorch the onions, about 4 minutes. Add the reserved mushroom stock, duck stock, reserved chopped smoked mushrooms, garlic, and thyme. Fold in the cooked beans and stir to combine. Cover tightly, transfer to the oven, and bake 1½ hours. Uncover and scatter the breadcrumbs over the top; continue baking , uncovered, until golden brown on top, another 30 minutes. Let cool slightly and serve directly from the pot, garnished with scallions.

Winter Curtido (*Curtido de Invierno*)

A *curtido* is a type of vegetarian pickled salad popular in Central America as food for Lent. Recipes can straddle a fine line between poached vegetables in mild salt broth and true pickles preserved in strong brine or vinegar. Generally, recipes can include whatever vegetables are on hand, making this a flexible, versatile preparation to extend a bountiful season or make the most of a spare larder. A *curtido* made during the fall harvest, when many summer vegetables are still available, can last in the refrigerator until late winter. While beets are often included, I have chosen to leave them out, since their color bleeds into the dish, and to showcase the flavor of the other vegetables. In this recipe, I have taken inspiration from a Honduran curtido colored yellow with annatto, using vegetables available even in February.

Makes 4 quarts

1 pound rutabaga, peeled and sliced into matchsticks

1 pound celeriac, peeled and sliced into matchsticks

1 pound carrots, peeled and shredded

1 pound green cabbage, cored and thinly sliced or shredded

¼ cup extra-virgin olive oil

1½ pounds onions, cut in half lengthwise and sliced paper-thin

1 cup dry white wine

1 teaspoon ground annatto (*achiote molido*)

2 teaspoons ground *ají amarillo* (see Note, page 134), cayenne, or ground hot pepper

2 tablespoons dried Greek oregano

3 garlic cloves, minced

8 fresh bay leaves

½ cup white wine vinegar

2 tablespoons sea salt or pickling salt

Minced cilantro leaves, for garnish

In a nonreactive stewing pan, heat 2 quarts spring water over medium heat until simmering. Add the rutabaga and poach until tender, 8 to 10 minutes. Using a slotted spoon or strainer, transfer the poached rutabaga to a large work bowl; keep water simmering. Add the celeriac and poach until tender, 8 to 10 minutes, then transfer to the bowl. Add the carrots to the simmering water and poach until tender, 10 to 12 minutes. Transfer the carrots to the bowl. Finally, return the poaching water to a simmer, if necessary, and add the cabbage. Poach until just tender, 6 to 8 minutes. Transfer the cabbage to the bowl, reserving the poaching water.

In a large (6- to 8-quart), nonreactive stewing pan, heat the olive oil over medium heat just until it begins to crackle, and add the onions. Stir, cover, and sweat just until softened, about 5 minutes. Add the poached vegetables and the reserved poaching water to the pan, plus 1 cup fresh spring water, the wine, annatto, ají amarillo, oregano, garlic, bay leaves, vinegar, and salt. Cover and stew over medium heat until all the vegetables are hot, 5 to 6 minutes.

Bring a large pot of water to a vigorous boil. Sterilize 4 1-quart jars and lids in the boiling water. While both are still hot, carefully transfer the vegetable mixture into the sterilized jars. Cover with the lid and close tightly, then let cool. Transfer to the refrigerator and keep up to 3 months.

REMEMBER THE SOUP BUNCH

A staple of frugal kitchens, a "soup bunch" is a practical bundle of aromatics and root vegetables added to vegetable (or meat) stock to brighten and deepen its flavor. Even during lean times, one could usually count on the larder or root cellar—today, the crisper drawer—for a carrot, parsnip, potato, or turnip; leeks, onions, or, in spring and summer, green onions; and fresh herbs and vegetables, such as dill, parsley, rosemary, or thyme and cabbage, celery, squash, or tomatoes. Tied together with kitchen twine like a bouquet garni, a soup bunch can be added to leftover vegetable-poaching liquid or fresh water and simmered into a serviceable stock. Added to commercial or homemade broth, a soup bunch contributes fresh, seasonal vegetable flavor that enlivens any recipe.

Today, both farmers markets and supermarkets commonly offer packaged combinations of aromatics, root vegetables, and herbs as soup bunches, tailored to local communities and regional specialties. While northern cities like Philadelphia had their own versions, soup bunches feature notably in Lowcountry cuisine and across the coastal South, with variations in New Orleans, Savannah, and famously, Charleston. The Charleston soup bunch traditionally comprised squash, celery, carrot, baby parsnips, green onions or scallions, dill, and thyme.

Tie sliced squash, aromatics, root vegetables, and fresh herbs together with kitchen twine. In a large pot, cover the soup bunch with stock or water. Bring to a boil over medium-high then reduce heat and simmer until reduced by one-third to one-half. Strain stock, discard solids, and use the enhanced stock as desired.

Garden Parables in Shades of Green

There are many practical reasons for keeping a garden diary; perhaps the most instructive and spiritual one being to interpret the poetry of life through plants. While the kitchen garden may seem still and silent to the casual observer, for the attuned gardener there is always a pulse of life that charges the air. Mother Nature always sets an example, sometimes orderly and teachable, at other times not always laid upon us with that same grace.

After reading *Le Potager d'un Curieux* [A Garden of Curiosities] (1892) by Nicolas-Auguste Paillieux and Désiré Bois, my inner Green Man was inspired to plant their enthusiastically described Oxalis Deppei for my book, *Heirloom Vegetable Gardening*, reissued in a new edition in 2018. What those venerable Frenchmen did not mention is that once you plant it you will always own it. Its cheerful pink flowers now bloom in every corner of Roughwood—not even the voles will touch it. My diary recorded its progress or, more accurately, its wild escape at the expense of vegetables far more useful. The same lesson applies to the Chinese yam (which is a rare tuber you can eat raw), somewhat deceptively known as Cinnamon Vine. While it may sound like costly floral material for the perfect wedding, it is in fact kudzu's shameless first cousin. On the other hand, the delightfully delicate crosnes are thriving (Paillieux and Bois gave the Asian tuberous betony its European name) and I have celebrated that success with a recipe (see page 156).

Perusing an old bookshop, I stumbled upon Louise Riotte's *Planetary Planting* (1972), which is all about organic gardening by the signs of the zodiac, or more accurately the basics of lunar agriculture. This is quite popular in some quarters of the garden world, and while this special niche of garden knowledge may seem peculiar, artificial, or overly dramatized, this is precisely how the Pennsylvania Dutch farmed for centuries; their almanacs are filled with detailed lunar instructions and zodiacal advice. By keeping such a diary, you may see for yourself whether there are correlations between the stars and what happens in your garden. Keeping it all organized on paper creates a system of reference that accumulates into something called experience. Eventually, you reach a point where you can answer questions and give advice; such as, what should I be doing in January?

On New Year's Day I follow the old Pennsylvania Dutch custom of blessing all the trees on the property. Each one gets three taps with a special healer's cane to bring good luck, to ensure the well-being of the tree in the coming year, and, if it is a fruit tree, that it will bear heavily. Trees are living beings that cannot move, so they must be protected. Lenape Indians watched over ancient chestnut trees in the area around what is now Roughwood because they understood the wisdom that flowed from centuries-old trees—and the chestnuts that provided them with food through the winter.

"January 4. Set seed in the greenhouse for Red Wethersfield onions, deer horn plantains, allium kurrat (Egyptian leeks), and Rat-Tailed Radishes, Purple Cut-Short Beans, Tick Beans, and transplanted Datil Peppers."

Adhering to the theme of a green diary, I water January seedlings in the greenhouse since I have already started tropical peppers and eggplants (always slow to germinate), and to start my onions, leeks, and early spring greens. These are the hardy plants that will go into the ground soonest after the thaw. On Valentine's Day, I start tomatoes, spring lettuces, the rest of the peppers, and cold-tolerant vegetables like cabbages and kales. None of these plants can go into the garden as seedlings otherwise slugs or rodents would eat them; the idea is to develop strong plants in the greenhouse, then move them outdoors once good weather and their hardiness permit.

"February 14. Set seed in the greenhouse for tomatoes: Green Zebra, Howard German, Hess, Pink Peach, Persimmon, Chalk's Early Jewel, and Tree Tomato; white African "Soxna" eggplant, Walloon Chicory, Forage Kale, and Lark's Tongue Kale."

March 17, St. Gertrude's Day. For the rest of America it's St. Patrick's Day, and while those other folks are wearing green and carousing; in Dutch Country, they're planting. Pennsylvania remains the third most important agricultural state in the nation, and claims the highest number of family farms selling directly to local consumers—over six thousand in 2019. So, we mark that date as the true beginning of spring with the ritual scattering of St. Gertrude Cake crumbs in the four corners of the garden, followed by planting potatoes, leeks, shallots, and cabbage, plus flowers for the Eckleit (garden fairies) to ensure a bountiful crop.

"March 20. Planted in the Celtic barley, Polish Wheat, Poulard wheat, Ungarische Schramayr Potato, All Red Potato, Gatersleben Potato, and Early Rose."

April Fool's Day is a good day for prognostication because the state of the weather will determine the pace of spring planting. Nearly thirty varieties of early potatoes go in first to be lifted in July—nothing like new potatoes for the kitchen! But there are times when we have had a surprise late-spring snowstorm, which we call "onion snow" in Pennsylvania because it is thought to benefit the onions we all have planted. Other times it has been so warm that the fruit trees bloom so early they then get hit by another surprise frost. One year it was so warm in April that we planted tomatoes on the 24th. Old-timers will warn you not to plant tomatoes until the end of May, but we got away with it. Tomatoes, eggplants, and other heat-loving vegetables won't thrive if the ground is cool or when the nights are cool and damp, so early planting has its risks. But that is perfect lettuce and pea weather, so it is important to have several planting schemes ready to take advantage of fickle weather.

The Lenape Indians have said that when the oak trees bud out and the leaves are the size of mouse ears, it's time to plant corn. If you plant corn too early it will rot in the ground. We often start it in the greenhouse, until it has grown perhaps ten inches tall, before we plant it outside. This gives the stalks a head start and allows us to stagger plantings so that we can have four varieties in the same garden without them crossing.

"May 10. Planted in the garden: Lime Basil, Round Eggplant, Huberschmidt Ground Cherry, Verde Claro eggplants, White Scimitar Pea, Yellow Jersey Sweet Potato, D'Avignon Long Radish, Black Brandywine Tomato, Vaux's Self-Folding Lettuce, and Victoria Rhubarb."

May is the serious month for planting. Late summer peas, cucumbers, squash—everything must go in the ground, including tomatoes (we usually plant 40 varieties) and our entire dahlia collection, to develop healthy roots before the onslaught of summer heat. Good root systems help reduce the need to water, especially if the plants are mulched with straw or salt hay. By the end of the month, we have begun planting the pole beans first, since they take the longest to ripen for seed saving. This means they are vulnerable to early frosts, so it is important to record in your journal exactly when the last frost of spring occurred and when the fall frosts are likely. This gives you your window of opportunity for the garden and can define the kind of garden you're able to plant. For instance, I would avoid lima beans if you live in New England—most summers are too short and the nights too chilly, making it extra difficult for vines to bear crops.

Bean Day on June 6 and the Strawberry Moon often occur within the same week. In Pennsylvania Dutch country, this was the day on the calendar that reminded you to get the rest of the beans planted, otherwise they will not make it through the first frost, which at Roughwood normally occurs around November 10. The Strawberry Moon was also an event for Native American celebrations of the wild-harvest strawberries, of course, and dishes made with Strawberry Corn, which is pink, and one of my favorite heirloom varieties. By the middle of June, we begin harvesting peas, garlic, and the late lettuces. If the weather is warm, we will also have a few tomatoes by the Fourth of July.

"June 22. Dug Early Rose potatoes—nice crop! Planted Coco Noir Bush Beans. Taught a workshop for 15 Temple University students and their professor. They weeded until 8 PM."

The height of summer for us is that sunny stretch between July 15 and August 15, when the days turn tropical. This is when hot-weather vegetables thrive and harvesting begins in earnest, as farm stands all over Pennsylvania can attest. Those without gardens can spend their entire weekends happily exploring country roads, just to find unusual produce freshly picked. Happily, prepared gardeners need only follow the brick walk leading from the kitchen.

"June 30. Planted in the garden Willow Leaf Lima, harvested peas: Lancashire Lad, Glory of England, and several fava beans."

There is something so magical about the full moon in August. Almost overnight the tomatoes begin to ripen. Some farmers claim it's the reflected sunlight off the moon; others say the light does something to the air and the tomatoes read it as a signal to hurry up because the next full moon could spell frost. Whatever the true reason, August is a busy time harvesting seeds or produce for the kitchen.

"August 15. Harvested all the Tutelo Strawberry Corn, about 3 bushels of ears for drying, selecting the best for seed, the culls for cornmeal. Delaware Indian Puhwem flour corn is setting tassels at about 16 feet."

September wind is always cool, and it gets cooler the closer we approach the actual first day of autumn. Such breezes may provide a welcome relief to the dog days of August, but they also come when late blight and powdery mildew can overtake the garden almost overnight. We generally clear the beds of summer crops to begin the next cycle.

"September 19. Planted fall vegetables for the winter garden: Radishes—Green Meat, Round Black Spanish, Violet de Gournay, and Watermelon; Hinona Kabu turnips, Petrowski turnips, mizuna (3 colors), Katie's Mustard Lettuce, Haldenstein Winter Spinach, Swabian Winter Peas, and Landis Winter Lettuce."

If we are lucky to get through the normal dip in temperatures at the end of September, then warm weather bounces back and we roll into Indian Summer all the way to Thanksgiving. But sometimes Mother Nature plays a different card from her hand and one must always think ahead:

"October 8. Made green tomato chutney from the fruit pulled off the vines in preparation for possible frost. All the peppers were pulled as well."

"October 12. Strange movement in the air above Roughwood. A pillar of frost formed over the garden, like a funnel cloud except that the sparkling dew swirled downward covering the Pretzel Beans and Cypriot melons with hoarfrost. Nothing else was touched."

"November 20. Worked in the garden lifting the dahlia collection. Potted up Variegata di Castelfranco radicchio. Planted a ridge of St. John's Shallots, and harvested the last of the rhubarb as well as the baby leeks that reseeded from last year's crop."

By St. Nicholas Day (December 5) most of the winter garden should be planted, but with a large dahlia collection, there is also plenty of work to do indoors.

"December 12. A volunteer helped tag, bag, and box the dahlias. Once the garden warmed up in the afternoon, we planted garlics: Rosewood, Metechi, Maxatawny, Freeville, Red Rezan, Belarus, Red Tochliavri, Chengdu, and Rocambole of Samarkand. While planting the Chengdu garlic, we found a few Papa Chaco seedling potatoes, which we salvaged for next year's garden."

"December 26. The Pennsylvania Dutch call this Second Christmas, and to commemorate the day, the sauerkraut from the November 6 cabbage harvest was ready to eat. Packed it up in ziplock bags and froze it, roughly 10 pounds. Kept back a quantity for a mess of pork and kraut on New Year's Day, this to bring Roughwood good luck in the coming year."

Sources

Seed for all varieties of heirloom vegetables named in this book can be sourced from The Roughwood Seed Collection, **roughwoodtable.org**.

Trustworthy suppliers (some of whom also source from Roughwood) include Baker Creek Heirloom Seeds, **rareseeds.com**; J. L. Hudson, Seedsman, **jlhudsonseeds.net**; Rancho Gordo, **ranchogordo.com**; Southern Exposure Seed Exchange, **southernexposure.com**; and Sow True Seed, **sowtrueseed.com**.

We are advocates of family farming and supporting local economies and foodways. The best source for fresh heirloom vegetables will likely always be your local farmers market. Farmers and growers across the country (who may also get seed from Roughwood) are the best folk to ask about heirlooms and the best ways to grow and use them. Cultivate relationships with friends and neighbors who grow herbs and vegetables in allotments or backyards. Sharing ideas and information, not to mention seeds, bumper crops, and homemade foods, is how local foodways are created.

Most cities today are lucky enough to have Asian, Indian, and Latin American grocers serving the local community. These can be great sources for heirloom vegetables that may prove hard to find in supermarkets, as well as international ingredients, seasonings, and staples—plus the opportunity for information and insight into those cultures.

Smoked mushrooms remain one of the ingredients we've come to love most at Roughwood but do not make. We asked one of our local growers, Heather McMonnies, to achieve the balance between delicate mushroom flavor and smoke, and she got it. Find more information at The Food Hedge.

Index

(Page references in italics refer to illustrations.)

greens:
  early spring, in Saint Gertrude's
    Day Salad with Rhubarb
    Dressing, 19–20
  Sunchoke Schales, 183
  see also collard(s)
Grigson, Jane, 8
Guarani, 64, 94

H

halloumi cheese, in Garlic Scape
  Sauté, *60*, 61
Ham and Bean Gravy, Parched
Corn Waffles with, *166*, 167–68
Haricot Petit Carré, 17
  Bean Soup with Salsify and
    Oyster Mushrooms, 14–16, *15*
hazelnuts, in Buckwheat Nut Cake,
  116, *117*
hominy:
  Cucumber Soup with, 54, *55*
  white, or *morocho partido*, 159
hot pepper(s):
  Aji Blanco Cristal, 66, 67
  Chipotle, Pickled Carrots with,
    78, *79*
  fish pepper, 96
  Green Corn Stew with Linguine,
    66
  Jam, 69
  Peruvian Pepperpot (*Soppa de
    Aji Amarillo*), 134

I

Indian Removal Act of 1830, 46
Irish Potato Cakes (*Pratie Oaten*),
  162
Iroquois, 46
Iroquois Bean Bread, 163

J

jams:
  Coztomotl, 68
  Hot Pepper, 69
  Pink Tomato, Thai-Style, 99
Jane Grigson's Vegetable Book
  (Grigson), 8
Jujubes, Pickled Green, 128, *129*

K

Kashmiri Collard Chutney, 122
Kievé, Squash, 94

L

Landreth, David, 173
Lemon Blush Pie, *70*, 71
Lenape Indians, 46
lentils, in Armenian Stuffed
Fermented Cabbage, 152–55
Lettuce with Spring Peas,
  Stir-fried, *38*, 39
lima beans:
  Pennsylvania Succotash, *170*, 171
  Tarbes Cassoulet with Smoked
    Mushrooms, 188
  Linguine, Green Corn Stew with,
    66
louvana, *24*, 25
  Grass Pea Omelet, 25
lovage, 48

M

Mapuche, 73
marinades:
  Crosnes and Radish, 156, *157*
  Ginger, 178
marmalades:
  Carrot, 50, *51*
  Green Corn, 62, *63*
masa harina:
  Allegheny Fardel Cakes, 110, *111*
  corn varieties for, 64
  Iroquois Bean Bread, 163
  Mohawk Corn Muffins, 161
  Nantucket Corn Cake, 165
  Squash *Kievé*, 94
  Wandering Spirits Tamales,
    144–46, *145*
  Xochipilli Tamales, 100–102, *101*
  Yellow Mole, 104
Mbombo beans, *139*
  Refried, with Plantains, 138
McMahon, Bernard, 28
Merkén, *72*, 73
  Sauce, 73
Merrell, Darrell, 90
Mexican (cooking):
  Chapalote Popcorn Roast, *118*, 119
  Pipián of Pumpkin Seeds and
    Baby Peanuts, 131

Wandering Spirits Tamales,
  144–46, *145*
  Xochipilli Tamales, 100–102, *101*
Mi'kmaq, 159
Miso, Squash Blossom, Pumpkin
  Dumplings in, *84*, 85
Mitchel, Maria, 165
Mohawk Corn Muffins, 161
Mole, Yellow, 104
Mongolian Sorghum Chapatis with
  Saffron, 143
Muffins, Mohawk Corn, 161
mushroom(s):
  chicken of the woods, 108, 120,
    121
  Chicken of the Woods, Soup, 120
  Oyster, Bean Soup with Salsify
    and, 14–16, *15*
  Smoked, Green Glaze Collards
    with Choclo and, 176
  Smoked, Tarbes Cassoulet with,
    188
Muskmelon, Wild, Chutney, 95

N

Nantucket Corn Cake, 165
Narragansett Succotash, *124*, 125
National Cook Book (Peterson), 27
Native Americans, 46, 64, 108, 151,
  159, 171, 197
  Mohawk Corn Muffins, 161
nettle:
  harvesting, 30
  leaves, in Stuffed Spinach Leaf
    Beets, 40, *41*
Tart, 30, 31
New England (cooking):
  Nantucket Corn Cake, 165
  Narragansett Succotash, *124*,
    125
New Guinea basil, 74, *75*
New Guinea Basil Pesto, 74

O

oat flour or oatmeal:
  Allegheny Fardel Cakes, 110, *111*
  Irish Potato Cakes (*Pratie
    Oaten*), 162
Omelet, Grass Pea, 25
one-pot meals:
  Armenian Stuffed Fermented
    Cabbage, 152–55

Acknowledgments

A book like this did not take shape without teamwork. I first want to thank Stephen Smith, the Roughwood Seed Collection Manager, for organizing all the ingredient grow-outs needed for the recipes and photography. His garden staff, especially Martha Madeira, must be commended for defying the summer rains and blistering heat to get things planted, weeded, and harvested. This applies as well to Matthew Gmitter, who looked the beast COVID-19 in the eye and won, all the while working in isolation to keep the seed harvest on track. Both of these amazing spirits have made certain that Roughwood and its visionary purpose remain in good hands.

Melissa Hancock, Grace Cooke, and Martha Sharples must be acknowledged for allowing us to use their respective properties in nearby Bryn Mawr, Pennsylvania, for many of the rare grow-outs needed for both seed production and the recipes. Their gracious generosity allowed us to generate enough seed to offer farmers and gardeners many of the rare heirlooms used in this book.

Heather McMonnies of Food Hedge Farm in Schwenksville, Pennsylvania, should receive special kudos for growing wild-card ingredients I needed for some of the recipes—Lemon Blush tomatoes, for example—and especially for saving the day with a fresh harvest of crosnes after we discovered that voles had decimated the patch at Roughwood. In spirit, I have dedicated the crosnes recipe on page 156 to Heather, who has given real meaning to the ancient message of St. Gertrude.

I also want to thank my dear friend Enrique Balladares for checking my Spanish and for the supply of rare seeds, cookbooks, and culinary inspiration he has given Roughwood following many travels through Central and South America. When the Dallett family owned Roughwood (1887–1910), they operated the Red D Line of sailing ships connecting Philadelphia to South America (I even have a menu from one of their steamers). So, in a sense, our friendship continues a long tradition of adventure, connection, and exchange linking Roughwood to exotic places.

I also want to thank my long-time friend and public relations manager, Valerie Andrew, who has spent many a summer evening sipping wine in the garden, helping with harvest, and sharing her critiques of new recipes and new flavors. At times she has been a perfect sous chef and personal sommelier. She has watched Roughwood grow and flourish, and it is an honor to dedicate this book to her.

Finally, but not the least, I want to thank my literary agent, Lisa Ekus, who really does believe in me and sometimes moves mountains to make way for my projects. She introduced me to Jono Jarrett, my editor at Rizzoli, who is highly gifted, a true editor in the classic and best sense of the word, indeed a rare talent in a publishing world turned upside down by forces other than literary merit. We have great fun when he comes to Roughwood with photographer Noah Fecks. They understand Roughwood's magic and I thank them both for allowing me to pour it into beautiful books.